DeepFake

You won't believe your eyes!

BOUSSAD ADDAD

Copyright © 2024 Boussad ADDAD

All rights reserved.

Warning

This book is a subtle blend of fiction and reality. Some facts, places, events and characters are authentic and faithfully described, while others are purely fictional or have been altered for the purposes of the story. Historical elements coexist with futuristic forecasts and science-fiction scenarios, albeit plausible in the near future. Real events, places and characters have been treated with care, but their interpretation may vary.

The opinions expressed by the characters do not necessarily reflect those of the author. Any resemblance to real people, living or dead, other than those explicitly mentioned, is purely coincidental.

Immerse yourself in this story, bearing in mind that the border between the real, the predictive and the imaginary is sometimes thinner than it seems.

"The darkest places in hell are reserved for the indecisive who remain neutral in times of moral crisis,

- Dante Alighieri

"Science without conscience is but the ruin of the soul",

- Rabelais

This book is dedicated to all the victims of unconsciousness.

Prologue: Inferno

Montreal, January 12, 1964.

For six hours now, M'hand and his son Lounis had been driving around in a Frontenac, a brand-new jewel he'd just bought for 2,500 Canadian dollars. Nothing could be more patriotic and popular than this car, with its maple leaf ornaments on the steering wheel and hubcaps. The snow-covered northern roads had made driving difficult, but now the car was speeding down Highway 25S, taking them towards southern Quebec. They would soon arrive at their destination, in the heart of Montreal's Ville-Marie district. Little Lounis, although exhausted, couldn't stop thinking.

- Dad, why go all this way to visit Mom?

- It's for her own good, darling. I went out of my way to make sure she was treated by a good doctor. She's now in the hands of the best doctor in America.

M'hand, with a touch of bitterness, continued in his accent from elsewhere, his words simple but powerful:

- My son, in the best of all possible worlds, this would be much simpler, almost on its own. Your mother sacrificed herself for her country, Canada. It's the least we owe her in return: good care. If I were the immigrant here, I wouldn't say anything. But this is her country, and she's given it everything.

- What exactly did she do?

- Do you know where I met your mother?

- Yes, in France. She told me that. She also told me that's where they gave you the three war medals hanging in the living room. She tells me a lot of things, you know, unlike you.

M'hand chose to ignore the last remark, which he knew to be correct, and continued with his explanation. He cleared his throat before continuing his tale, in a voice imbued with gravity.

- Here we are. It was during the war. The terrible Second World War. Your mom, as you know, was a nurse. As soon as she graduated, she chose to join the group of nurses accompanying the Allied armies during the Normandy landings in 1944. She was only nineteen at the time.

- Oh my God, she was so young, exclaimed the child, his eyes wide.

- Yes, but that was the norm in those troubled times. Even younger than that, you could join the army. War is an insatiable abyss, devouring men of all ages without ever satisfying itself.

- I can understand that. Dad, she also told me that your comrades in the French resistance nicknamed you Tintin. Is that really true?

The father smirked.

- Ah yes, Tintin was my nickname in the BCRA and the Marco-Polo network. But that's another long story. Let's get back to your mother. She had just become engaged - without getting married so she could enlist in the army - and set sail for Juno Beach in France. Crossing the Atlantic, she consulted the most recent list of Canadian casualties. There she discovered the name of her fiancé. Poor man, his fighter plane had been shot down over the Mediterranean and his body never recovered.

- You mean she had another man before you?

- Yes, but they hardly had time to live together. He was taken by the war too soon. She was devastated to discover his name among the dead. And that was only the beginning of her ordeal. Imagine the scenes of horror she had to face in the terrible Battle of the Bulge, the wounds she tried to heal. It had a profound effect on her, making her ill afterwards. I met her in the theater of battle, a few days before the end of the war. We were lucky enough to survive, unlike so many others. I think my presence helped her get through it. We supported each other, because I too had experienced my share of the apocalypse.

The father paused for a moment, staring into the past, before continuing.

- We managed to rebuild our lives and were lucky to have you and your sister. Unfortunately, her nightmares of war have never stopped. She often wakes up screaming, exhausted by these horrific visions. Ah, look, we've arrived at the hospital.

The child looked up at the building.

- Dad, it looks like a castle. It is beautiful.

M'hand preferred to remain silent, letting the words dissolve in the heavy air. "Appearances kill," he murmured so quietly that even the son beside him couldn't hear him. After a moment's reflection, he added:

- This psychiatric hospital was once a large villa. It belonged to a rich man, says M'hand, careful not to reveal any more than that.

***

Ravenscrag House, named after its position on a hill once inhabited by crows, was built in an Italianate style, following the austere yet elegant principles of Victorian architecture. Built between 1861 and 1863, this majestic residence was the work of Sir Hugh Montagu Allan, an influential Scottish banker and businessman. In 1940, he donated the property to the Royal Victoria Hospital. Since 1943, the building has housed the Allan Memorial Institute, integrating the psychiatry department of the hospital and the McGill University Health Centre.

M'hand and his son Lounis passed through a small, almost invisible gate, concealed within a monumental grille that surrounded a vast estate of several hectares. They entered the gardens of the institute, but still had a long drive of almost a hundred meters to go before finally reaching the sumptuous entrance to the hospital.

They were there at last. On either side of the door, two majestic columns, worthy of the grandest Roman temples, supported a pediment richly decorated with flowers and plants. At its center, a carved dog's head surmounted the Latin inscription "Spero", meaning "Hope". This institute was supposed to restore hope to broken souls.

M'hand had been filled with this sense of optimism since the day he had brought his wife to this place, far from suspecting the events to come. With determined steps, he made his way down a huge corridor, before turning left and starting up the stairs to the patient rooms. The place was strangely quiet, as if deserted by its occupants.

Suddenly, the eerie silence was broken by a faint sound resembling a shriek. M'hand wasn't sure what he'd heard. Perhaps an illusion to soothe his mind, unaccustomed to such a sensory void. Especially as his son, usually talkative, remained mute. But as they went on, this single cry multiplied, becoming distinct cries, resonating in this immense space like the body of a gigantic wind instrument. However, the melody here was synonymous with dread, capable of scaring off the most reckless.

M'hand, for all his life's achievements, suddenly felt overwhelmed by doubt, not exactly reassured. Memories of the war, with its trail of screams and suffering, rose to the surface. His terrified son clung to him, seeking in vain a comfort that M'hand himself struggled to find.

A nurse appeared in the distance, running in their direction. Panic-stricken, she shouted: "They've run away, they've run away, they've run away...".

When they reached a secondary corridor, father and son saw two nurses grabbing a man and dragging him back to the main hospital aisle. Wearing a helmet like all the patients here, he was shouting at the top of his voice: "Let me go, let me go, I don't want to be here anymore, I don't want to stay here anymore...". He was clearly one of the fugitives the nurse was talking about. M'hand and Lounis stepped aside to let the three men pass, when suddenly, in one swift movement, the patient head-butted one of the nurses. His helmet flew off and crashed to the floor. The noise of the impact added to an already unbearable din. M'hand continued on his way, still holding his son's hand in his own. His wife Hélène's bedroom was not far off. He pressed on. Just a few more meters to "find refuge there", he thought. In the meantime, M'hand glanced left and right at every room he came across. The first, the second, the third. They were all deserted, and each time he noticed the same thing: an empty bed and a headset on the floor, connected to a long cable spread out on the bed. It was connected to some kind of tape recorder, as big as a crate, with two large reels running.

Just a few more meters. M'hand was terrified he wouldn't find his wife. He ran, leaving his son a few steps behind.

*

Meanwhile, the World Congress of Psychiatry, bringing together doctors and psychiatrists from the four corners of the globe, was taking place just a stone's throw away, on the grounds of McGill University.

The Chairman stepped up to the podium, ready to introduce the day's guest of honor, the President of the World Psychiatric Association.

- Good morning, ladies and gentlemen, he began. Allow me to introduce our guest of honor for this second edition of the World Congress of Psychiatry, the celebrated, the famous, the brilliant Professor Donald Ewen Camerooooooooooooooooooooooon!

The packed amphitheatre erupted into thunderous applause.

Professor Cameron gave a speech that was intended to be historic:

- When I became a psychiatrist thirty years ago, I had ambitions to change the world. I was convinced that I was tackling the most hideous and least understood disease in the history of medicine. And I was going to make it happen. But, like all of us, I was confronted with the reality of mental illness. Many devastated families came to me, begging me to do something for their parents, their children, so that they could return home healed. I couldn't give them any assurances, but that's no longer the case. I can now look those parents in the eye and tell them that I will heal their children. Your dreams have come true again.

Here at the Allan Institute, we have introduced the first truly scientific treatment of mental illness in the history of medicine. The process has two phases: psychic control and deprogramming. It's a combination of the most basic common sense and the most advanced technology. We have solid evidence of healing in cases we once thought impossible. Let me give you an example: Hélène. A classic case of a depressive and suicidal person who had to spend the rest of her life in hospital. Now she's cured, symptom-free. She's ready to go out and join her loved ones. And Hélène is not alone. There are currently over a hundred, 104 to be precise, soon to be out of the woods. We have an exceptional 80% recovery rate. Yes, ladies and gentlemen, schizophrenia is no longer an incurable mental illness. I'm delighted to announce that we are currently conducting trials with the same protocol in several partner hospitals in Europe and Asia. Ladies and gentlemen, I ask you to raise your glasses in celebration of the birth of modern psychiatric hospitals.

Bravos rang out throughout the hall. The applause went on and on and on...

*

M'hand was there at last. He had arrived. Before he could relax and let his body breathe, he opened his mouth wide to inhale a breath of air. Paradoxically, he was suffocating, panicking. His wife wasn't there. He couldn't see her. Worse still, his sheets were full of blood. The helmet lay on the floor, far from the bed, near the doorway itself. The only living thing in the room were the spinning reels. M'hand was distraught and didn't know what to do. Not a nurse in sight to ask. But what had happened to Hélène? In a mechanical gesture, his brain almost turned off so he could think, he grabbed the headset and brought it close to his ear. A male voice came through. It went round and round: "When I get home, I'll be a good wife and a good mom", "When I get home, I'll be a good wife and a good mom", "When I get home, I'll be a good wife and a good mom" ...

M'hand let the helmet slip from his hands and crash to the floor with an inaudible crash, masked by the din in the hospital. He looked pale and didn't know what to think. He knew that Hélène had always been an admirable wife and mother. He didn't understand the meaning of this message, which should be playing over and over in his ears. He grabbed his son's hand and ran to get some information.

After wending his way through the maze, M'hand finally came across two nurses. He tried to question them.

- Do you know where the patient Mme Hélène Amrouche is, please?

The first answered before he'd even finished his sentence.

- Sorry, sir, we don't know. You'll have to check at reception.

It wasn't his habit, but M'hand got angry and raised his voice:

- But what kind of welcome are you talking about? There's nobody there.

The second nurse seemed to have a piece of information. She looked at her colleague and said:

- I think she's the patient from the "*sleeping room*".

- The patient Cerberus subjected to LSD and TEC?

- Yes, I think it's her.

M'hand understood nothing of what was being said and just listened. But who was Cerberus? What was LSD? And TEC?

The nurses had nicknamed the hospital's director, Professor Cameron, "Cerberus", in reference to the famous guardian of hell in Greek mythology. They felt the nickname suited him, given the hell that the psychiatric hospital had become. LSD was the substance he had just introduced into his memory-erasing protocol. He used a neuroleptic to plunge patients into a state of artificial coma for days, even months at a time. During this period, he administered a hallucinogen, LSD, and inflicted strong electric shocks to the brain. Then, he would expose them to sound messages designed to embed themselves in their minds and unconsciously guide them to modify their behavior according to the messages received. The sounds were played over and over again, for hours and days on end, inflicting psychological and physical torture. Even the strongest of patients eventually broke down.

The nurses pointed M'hand in the direction of the famous room before disappearing.

M'hand ran as best he could, pulling his son by the hand. When they arrived, they found the door closed. A small window at man-height would have allowed them to see what was going on in the room, but it was covered by a sheet of paper. M'hand knocked several times on the door, and a voice finally answered:

- Who's there?

- I'm the husband of Hélène, the patient.

A long silence ensued, leaving M'hand in a state of total incomprehension. The nurse spoke in a low voice, obviously addressing one or more of the colleagues beside her.

- Do you think we can let him come in and see?

- I don't know, but he's her husband anyway. He has the right.

- But look at her condition, she's...

- It's not our fault, it's Cameron's responsibility.

- Cerberus is considered a god, so he's safe.

- OK, I open. Come what may.

When the door opened, M'hand was literally stunned by the scene before him. He didn't even recognize his wife. Sitting on the bed, looking lost, her white clothes had turned red and were torn all over. Her face was scarred from top to bottom, unrecognizable. Blood dripped from her hands. She had obviously self-mutilated herself, ripping off whole chunks of her face. She repeated the same words over and over, barely intelligible: "Let me go, let me go...".

M'hand could hardly believe it was his beautiful Hélène standing in front of him. He was stunned and remained motionless for a long moment. A lifetime of happiness flashed before his eyes. He told himself it was all in the past and he'd never see it again.

Suddenly, as if waking from a deep sleep, he opened his eyes wide and looked around for his son. He found him crouched, back to the wall, in the fetal position. He was in shock, inert, his eyes riveted on his mother.

M'hand took him in his arms and covered his eyes so as not to see. But it was too late, this scene of horror would haunt the little boy for the next forty years...

Chapter 1

It had been three hours since the A320 Neo, fully loaded for the weekend, left Greece and flew peacefully over Europe. The sky was clear all the way, without the slightest hint of turbulence. The new-generation jet's engines hummed softly, a monotonous noise you soon got used to, and eventually forgot. Kenneth, exhausted by the long wait for his connecting flight to Athens, had no trouble drifting off to a restful sleep. But this rest was abruptly interrupted by the pilot's voice:

- Ladies and Gentlemen, we are about to begin our descent to Charles de Gaulle airport in Paris. Please return to your seats and fasten your seatbelts.

Although satisfied that he would soon reach his destination, Kenneth would have liked to have slept a little longer. He was dreaming of his new girlfriend, a striking encounter he had made in Greece, which was turning his life upside down and occupying his thoughts with a thousand amorous projects.

The stewardesses passed down the aisle, checking that each passenger was properly strapped in and that the hubcaps were up. Kenneth pulled his up, imitating a child sitting in front of him, obeying his mother without understanding why.

- It's for our own safety, darling, she replied gently.

Kenneth, in an inaudible whisper, mentally completed the explanation: "In the event of a problem, it's essential to see what's going on outside, to alert the crew or allow the rescue team to take a look inside. It also helps the eyes adapt to the light outside before disembarking."

- Ladies and gentlemen, prepare for landing.

The plane skimmed the runway, bouncing slightly before finally touching down. The sound of the wheels touching the ground was brief because of the bounce, but then became continuous, followed by the sound of the airbrakes deploying. The aircraft slowed rapidly before turning right towards the taxiway.

- Ladies and gentlemen, we have arrived at Paris Charles de Gaulle airport. Please remain seated and keep your seatbelts fastened until the aircraft has come to a complete stop and the warning lights have gone out. Make sure you don't forget anything before leaving the plane. It's a sunny day, so make the most of it. Thank you for choosing our airline, we hope to see you soon on our Air France KLM network.

After a few turns, the plane finally came to a halt near the gangway. The signals went out and the door opened, triggering a rush of passengers to their luggage.

Kenneth retrieved his bag and slipped into the queue, eager to be reunited with his beloved. With his European passport in hand, he chose the normally faster route for automatic document verification. After a few minutes of waiting in a seemingly endless queue, his turn finally arrived. With a sure, yet nervous gesture, he placed his passport on the scanner. He held his breath, waiting for the signal that would authorize his passage. But a relentless red glow lit up, accompanied by a strident beep. The door remained closed.

Incredulous, he took the passport back, flipped through it quickly, confirming that the page displaying his passport photo was indeed the one he'd presented. His heart beat faster as he carefully placed the document back on the scanner, taking care to align it perfectly. The heart-rending sound of refusal was heard again. The barrier remained stubbornly closed, like a stone sentry.

- Hold on, please, I'm on my way, said a customs officer, moving towards Kenneth.

Kenneth let the other passengers pass and waited for the agent to arrive. What's going on? he asked himself. The Brexit had already caused problems on his last trip, when his Scottish identity card had been refused. Now he had a passport, but that too seemed to be a problem.

- Hello, sir, we need to do some checking. May I see your passport, please?

- What checks?

- You'll see. Do you have any hold luggage to collect?

- Yes, two suitcases.

- Don't worry about it. Just follow me, please.

Kenneth's concern grew as he followed the officer through the airport's labyrinthine corridors to a small room where three other policemen were waiting. The officer handed the passport to a colleague, nodding.

- Hello, sir, are you Kenneth Lewis?

- Yes.

- Are you a lawyer in Paris?

- Yes.

- Please turn around and hold out your hands. You are under arrest for premeditated murder.

Kenneth tried to protest, but the handcuffs were already closing around his wrists.

- I'm sorry, Mr. Lewis, but you'll have to explain yourself to the judge. You can make a phone call and get a lawyer.

Kenneth's world collapsed. Dizzy, he couldn't understand what was happening to him. His dreams, his plans with his new companion, all seemed to vanish. Now he had to concentrate on defending himself.

Chapter 2

Two months earlier...

The Herald offices were deserted. Dihya used to have everything at her fingertips, but now she had to walk dozens of meters to reach her colleagues. The reorganization of the newspaper, following a massive redundancy plan, was still pending. A move was planned, but not imminent. For the time being, the priority was to cover a burning issue: artificial intelligence, which was revolutionizing all sectors at dizzying speed. Every day brought its share of surprises, breathtaking innovations in every field, but also spectacular company collapses, sometimes involving historic giants thought to be untouchable.

Dihya had a scoop, and she was buzzing with excitement. She knew she'd hit the big time with her second tech scoop in less than a month. Social networks would be abuzz, and her name would be at the top of the most relayed hashtags.

Her first article, published three weeks earlier, focused on Octopus, formerly OpenAI. Forced to change its name two years ago, this behemoth no longer had anything to do with the original organization, which advocated opening up its computer programs to the AI community. The term "Open" had literally become an embarrassment. Dihya's scoop revealed the imminent dismantling of the company as a result of the Antitrust Act. Octopus, which had succeeded in burying giants like Google, was now worth more than all the other GAFAs combined, with a valuation of twenty trillion dollars, exceeding the GDP of the European Union. Now systemic, hundreds of thousands of companies depended on its artificial intelligence technology. A cyber-attack on Octopus could trigger a global economic crisis worse than that of 2008. The US authorities had deemed it prudent to split Octopus into several specialized entities. Dihya's first scoop shook the world of technology and finance.

Her new scoop concerned Octopus again, in a logical follow-up since it touched on security. The Board of Directors was about to announce a collective resignation following a major disagreement with the CEO over the deployment of the latest version of their AI. For them, this AI posed a serious security problem: it had managed to transfer itself to other machines by replicating itself like a computer virus. Prudence dictated that this AI should not be deployed with an opening onto the Internet, but the CEO disagreed.

The title of the article Dihya was about to publish was interrogative, but clear to insiders: "Octopus, the Daedalus that forgot to chain its machines?" Dihya appreciated metaphorical and mysterious titles, which created strong mental images and pushed readers to immerse themselves in her writing. Those who knew her knew that there was always something to learn, even outside her main subject.

A historian by training, Dihya possessed several degrees and an extraordinary culture. After teaching at various universities, including Harvard and Yale, she turned to investigative journalism. Her boundless curiosity and persuasive techniques made her a formidable journalist. Stubborn and reckless, she never let herself be intimidated, even in the face of the worst threats. Her new target was Octopus, and she was determined to fight it to the bitter end, despite the constant pressure. The company had become *too big to attack*, but Dihya was determined.

Chapter 3

Dihya had spent a grueling day at the Herald. The frantic pace of her tasks had left little room for reflection, each moment filled with a new urgency, her article to finish, an impromptu meeting. As she drove through the streets of Paris, now plunged into darkness, she let herself relax in the comfort of her car, seeking a well-deserved respite. The engine hummed softly, accompanying her thoughts as they wandered far from the hustle and bustle of the newsroom.

With a mechanical gesture, she turned on the radio, hoping that the airwaves of France Culture would offer her a few minutes of peace, a cultural interlude, perhaps a piece of classical music or a literary analysis that would help her release the accumulated tension. But no sooner did the deep, familiar voice of the presenter emerge from the speakers than Dihya felt her heart clench. The words echoing in the cabin brought her back to reality, bringing to mind the subject that haunted her thoughts, the insidious problem that refused to leave her in peace. Once again, fate was playing tricks on her, transforming this moment of relaxation into an inevitable confrontation with her deepest anxieties.

🔊 Welcome to France Culture. We're back for another episode of our new program devoted to the digital world. Today's episode is entitled: "All trapped in Musk's net?"

In this age of ubiquitous connectivity, nowhere on this planet - be it the depths of the Amazon, the vast expanses of the Sahara or the remote islands of the Pacific - goes unnoticed. The worldwide Starlink network ensures a seamless connection to civilization. All airlines have entered into partnerships with Elon Musk's empire, ensuring uninterrupted Internet connectivity even in mid-flight. The Web now lives up to its name, as the entire planet is enveloped in its network. This connectivity even extends beyond, with links already established to the Moon and soon to Mars.

The entire telecoms sector has been turned upside down. No need to buy a phone chip or a credit card. With the smartphone X, the latest technological marvel from Musk's teams, all applications are superfluous. Whatever the need, just say it out loud. To make a purchase, all you have to do is say what you want. To transfer money to a loved one, nothing could be simpler: indicate the amount and the recipient. A quick validation and the money instantly appears in the recipient's account. Traditional currencies such as the Euro and the Dollar have all but disappeared, replaced by *X-coins*, the digital currency of the X network. Elon Musk has not only created a universal application, he has also given birth to the X-Universe. The world now revolves around this network.

Elon Musk has taken a stunning revenge on history despite the hostilities that have built up around his person, particularly since he drew closer to the Republican Party. Here's a look back at his extraordinary career:

In 1999, Elon Musk founded X.com with the ambition of revolutionizing online payments. Despite rapid growth, X.com faced many challenges and fierce competition. In March 2000, X.com merged with Confinity, a company offering a similar payment service called PayPal. Internal conflicts led to Musk's dismissal in favor of Peter Thiel as CEO in October 2000. Thiel renamed the company PayPal in 2001, focusing exclusively on online payments.

PayPal flourished, particularly on eBay, and went public in July 2002. Shortly afterwards, eBay acquired PayPal for $1.5 billion. PayPal's success cemented its place in the fintech industry, thanks in large part to Musk's initial vision and investments.

Years later, Musk's attachment to the letter X remained intact. He bought the X.com domain in 2017 and used the X in various projects, including SpaceX and the Tesla Model X. He even named his son "X Æ A-12". This affinity culminated in Twitter's rebranding as X, marking the beginning of the shaping of the X-Universe.

In this hyper-connected world, people spend literally almost all their time online. Disconnection is impossible, even during sleep. The many gadgets worn on the body, *wearables*, measure various bodily activities such as heart rate and temperature, transmitting this data to analysis systems for a comprehensive report. This makes it possible to detect any present or future malfunctions. This is the age of predictive medicine.

Outside of sleep hours, brains are immersed in a new universe where humans and machines cohabit, often indiscriminately. A world of dreams and escapism, a refuge from everyday worries. A world where digital soup is always hot, served politely and persuasively. Mental obesity has become the world's most widespread disease.

In the face of this scourge, or to ease one's conscience as is customary in the world of digital platforms, the X phone, like other smartphones for that matter, allows you to program a total disconnection from the Internet, a *shutdown* with no possibility of reactivation. The only way to re-establish the connection is to ask a third party, a guardian angel designated when the *shutdown* was programmed. Social pressure being strong, no reasonable person would dare ask for this without a serious pretext. Imagine having to call your best friend to reconnect you to the Internet, as if you needed your fix of digital heroin! You wouldn't...

= =

Dihya couldn't let the show go any further, preferring to turn off the radio. Her overheated brain was on the verge of implosion.

Chapter 4

Despite her prowess, Dihya was feeling a growing sense of unease in her daily routine. Tension was mounting between her and the Herald's new editor-in-chief, with whom every article became a fierce battle. Pressure to censor sensitive subjects was mounting from all sides. The wave of redundancies, which had swept away many allied colleagues, was undermining her morale.

As part of her investigative work, Dihya spent endless hours on the Internet, scouring social networks for contacts and information. Publishing an article was only the first step; after that, you had to create maximum online engagement. Controversy was often the weapon of choice, but it came at a high cost. Dihya had to monitor reactions, respond to criticism - which was sometimes orchestrated by well-organized groups, such as political parties. Coordinated attacks turned into an avalanche of hatred, often involving harassment and physical threats. It was a vicious circle: the more she responded, the more attacks came. This dynamic drained her of energy, both physical and mental.

Although nicknamed Xena at the Herald, Dihya eventually broke down. Paradoxically, she was spending even more time online, binge-watching series on Netflix until dawn. She had become a true digital *junky*, addicted to the glow of screens from morning to night.

Aware that her health was at stake, a solution had to be found. Like many of her colleagues, she opted for a stay in a digital detox center. These establishments, which had appeared en masse in recent years, thrived on digital malaise. Innovative, these stays were now held abroad, without any Internet connection, the responsibility for digital isolation being transferred to the center. Some even included accommodation with local families, strictly instructed never to provide their guests with the WIFI code.

For premium stays, dream destinations were on offer: from the Moroccan desert to immersion in the Amazon, or even a total isolation on an island cut off from the world. For Dihya, the choice fell on a place rich in history, in tune with her personality: the island of Crete, in Greece.

Chapter 5

Kenneth strode confidently down the dark and imposing corridor of the courthouse. Each step echoed his recent victory, a triumphant acquittal of a man accused of murder, adding another star to his already impressive record. Night had already been spreading its thick veil over the city for several hours. Kenneth's black robe shifted in the darkness, giving him a spectral allure as he made his way to his car parked in the courthouse surface parking lot. His head alone caught the pale light of a distant street lamp, making the scene almost unreal.

This supposedly secure area was not without a certain amount of anxiety for Kenneth, who always felt vulnerable in this isolated space. The underground parking lot was even more sinister, and he avoided it as much as possible. Justice, he knew, was not a world populated by angels. Every disappointed customer or angry relative represented a potential danger, a threatening shadow in this world of justice and injustice.

As he drove home, Kenneth's thoughts were interrupted by an illuminated billboard advertising a holographic concert by a pop star at Bercy Arena. Technology had progressed so much that it was now almost impossible to distinguish a hologram from a real person. For spectators, it became a game of guessing the real or fictitious presence of the artist on stage. The panel made Kenneth think of his daughter, who was passionate about music and taking violin lessons at the conservatory. She was due to perform this evening at a small party organized at the town hall church to raise funds for a charity. He had promised to attend, but his professional obligations had once again forced him to cancel. Feeling remorseful, Kenneth ordered his voice assistant:

- Siri, call my daughter.

Instantly, the artificial intelligence executed. His daughter's name appeared on the screen, and the ringtone sounded. But no one picked up. Voicemail was triggered, and Kenneth asked to call back. Once again, the ringing sounded, then stopped abruptly. She'd hung up. The voicemail took over, but Kenneth wanted to hear his daughter's voice, to speak to her directly. Lost in thought and overwhelmed by sadness, he knew this was a difficult situation for both of them. Just as he was about to start the call again, a ding sounded. A message had just arrived:

Stop calling me. You're going to tell me the same thing you told me about the school party you missed. You never keep your promises and you never will...

Kenneth felt that the situation was getting out of hand, with no solution on the horizon. He loved his daughter deeply, but also his work, and couldn't imagine any other career. Short of going back in time and making other decisions, there was no way out. The burden of his work had already cost him his marriage. His wife had left him for another man, and now his daughter was inexorably drifting away from him. In the past, he could at least see her when he came home in the evening, but those days were gone. Now all he had left were a few scattered weekends, a few fragments of vacation to spend with her. His solitude gnawed at him.

To escape this slump, Kenneth had plunged into writing. He devoted himself entirely to it, finding in it a precious escape. He spent his days off, his weekends, all his free time, writing about a subject close to his heart. It was his own way of giving meaning to his life, of combating his growing isolation.

Chapter 6

Twenty floors below ground, the bunker was plunged into total darkness. Not a ray of sunlight could penetrate the wall of darkness. Life in this underground sanctuary wasn't paradise, but for Tarakna, it was a haven of peace. He felt at home here. Silence reigned supreme, the only light coming from the computer screens surrounding him. Despite this, he wore headphones on his head, not to listen to music, but to further isolate himself from the outside world, creating an absolute vacuum in his ears. An antenna on the surface connected him to the Internet, his only link with civilization. A fragile link, but one whose ramifications could shake the entire world.

Tarakna lived alone. The untimely loss of his father had scarred him forever, and he had never really been able to get over it. He left school early, taking refuge in the world of computers. Two fields fascinated him: artificial intelligence and psychology. He wanted to master them at all costs. As soon as he got home from his job as a waiter in a restaurant, he would immerse himself in books and articles on these subjects, with a marked preference for AI at first. Over the years, he had become a true expert, creating programs far more advanced than those designed by engineers at prestigious companies. His skills had enabled him to found several startups, which he sold for huge sums. He had become rich enough never to need to work again.

But money hadn't dimmed his obsession with building a digital clone of his late father, a so-called *ghostbot*. He wanted to dialogue with him, to find answers to questions that had haunted him since childhood.

To verify the feasibility of his project, Tarakna needed optimal conditions: a massive quantity of good quality data. So, he posted an advertisement on the Internet:

==================================

We're looking for volunteers for a unique experiment to create the perfect digital clone. Participants will be asked to provide all their personal data, including texts, SMS messages, videos and photos. They will also answer questionnaires specially designed for this experiment. Their voice will be recorded as they read a text constructed for the same purpose. Facial videos with various expressions will also be taken from different angles.

Volunteers will take part in the evaluation of the clone for one month, for four hours a day. One year after the end of the experiment, all data collected will be destroyed. Each participant will receive $15,000 in compensation, and the clone - in the form of a computer program - will be offered to them if they wish.

NB: preference will be given to those who provide the most data, including access to their social network accounts, browsing history, etc.

= =

As soon as the ad was published, Tarakna's inbox was flooded with messages...

Chapter 7

Every time Kenneth crossed the threshold of his home, he couldn't help thinking of his ex-wife, who used to cheerfully call out "Is that you, Kenny?" whenever she heard the doorbell in the evening. Now, only a heavy silence greeted him, and the echo of that gentle female voice echoed only in the depths of his mind. After setting down his belongings, he took a quick shower, then dropped onto the sofa in the living room. Exhausted, he knew he had to get up without delay to continue writing his book.

Kenneth had little time to savor a moment's respite. He quickly warmed up a box of pasta, swallowed it almost mechanically and headed for his office. He was in the home stretch; only a few final touches remained before he could send his manuscript to the publisher. This first book, which he had been working on for two years, represented much more than a simple literary project: it was a real personal commitment.

Entitled "The Code", the book retraced the tribulations and complete history of the Nuremberg Code, from its earliest inspirations, such as the Hippocratic oath dating back to Antiquity, to its final elaboration for the Nazi trial in 1946. Contrary to what many might have thought, the Nuremberg Code was not just a deontological or ethical text. It was also a crucial legal document, used to condemn the Nazis in a trial under international law. Kenneth, a lawyer by profession, felt fully justified in tackling this complex subject.

But his motivations were also personal. He dedicated this book to his grandfather, to whom he devoted an entire chapter. His grandfather, one of the most respected doctors of his time, had been called in to help assess the psychiatric condition of Rudolf Hess, Adolf Hitler's staunch political companion since the 1920s and his minister since 1933. The diagnosis of the doctor and his colleague - "hysterical amnesia" - had saved Hess's life, averting his execution. This amnesia turned out to be feigned a few years later.

Rudolf Hess lived to 93, dying by hanging in 1987. From 1966 until his death, he was the sole occupant of Spandau prison, at an exorbitant cost to West Germany. The Allied forces had wanted to maintain this prison and its sole occupant as a symbol of their alliance. Kenneth saw another meaning in this: he was immensely proud of his grandfather, who had judged Hess without animosity or vengeance. This had enabled mankind to preserve, for a long time, a witness to Nazi atrocities, reminding all those who would forget the horrors of the past. And it offered yet another argument, if one were needed, that the death penalty no longer has a place among civilized mankind.

Chapter 8

Hundreds of responses flooded into Tarakna's inbox in the space of a few hours. Yet, determined not to rush his decision, he gave himself a week to sort through the applications. Some candidates were just looking for the money, and that, he knew, would never work. His approach was almost scientific: it was necessary to invest oneself totally, to believe in the idea, to set off as if on a mission.

After a meticulous pre-selection process, twenty candidates were called for interview. In the end, three men and two women were selected, each with a unique psychological profile that clearly set them apart from the others. As instructed, each candidate provided all available personal data. To simplify the task, they provided a copy of their computer hard drive and telephone. Social network account histories were also downloaded. A program designed by Tarakna was used to clean up this data and retain only the essentials.

The second phase was crucial, and involved answering specific questions based on the OCEAN (or Big Five) model, which was used to psychologically profile a person. The classic method involved answering multiple-choice questions (MCQs), which were used during pre-selection to identify a representative of each OCEAN model type. In this case, subjects dialogued with a chatbot and answered as naturally as possible. At times, these were thinking problems, at others, situational challenges. To reduce response noise, i.e. inadvertent or deliberate deviations, the same questions were rephrased and asked several times. This made it possible to verify a personality trait. A neurotic person (the N in OCEAN) frequently changes mood and gets irritated easily. On the third repetition of the same question, such a person would become irritated and show it in their answers. An extrovert (letter E from OCEAN) feels at ease surrounded by people, unlike an introvert. In this case, the chatbot could simulate a crowded place where all eyes were riveted on a specific point and say "You're in the middle of these people and everyone is looking at you." The subject's reaction would then be revealing. Indeed, the subjects were filmed, enabling an emotion-recognition AI to analyze their facial and body expressions, correlating their words and gestures. Psychological profiling thus became extremely complete.

By the end of the collection, five titanic databases had been built up. All that remained was to use them to train an AI, a gigantic neural network, a kind of clone that could reproduce them. Tarakna named his program Asklepios, after the Greek god of medicine who raised the dead. He could ask his chatbot anything, including raising the dead!

Once the clones had been built, Tarakna set up a simple protocol to evaluate them. He asked the same questions simultaneously to the subject (the real person) and his clone, synchronizing their responses. If the answers provided were semantically close enough, then the clone was faithful to the original. This process was fully automated thanks to synchronization.

After this initial assessment, Tarakna identified situations where the clones had failed by reacting very differently from their original. He would then replay the scenario in the presence of the subject and question him on what could explain the discrepancy. Most of the time, this was due to the absence of a crucial piece of information in the training database. This was then added. Gradually, the gaps were corrected, filling in the gaps before re-training Asklepios.

By the end of the fourth iteration, all the clones had been perfected. Their performance was extraordinary. With each question, it was difficult to distinguish the copy from the original. Tarakna was ecstatic.

He could now move on to the next phase of his plan...

Chapter 9

Kenneth had finally published his book, a literary triumph. Rave reviews were pouring in from the media. Even the 8 p.m. news on a national TV channel mentioned it in connection with a related subject: the publication of a book across the Atlantic that disputed the death of Rudolf Hess by suicide, thus reviving the assassination theory.

Kenneth's book set off a storm on the Web and beyond. Reactions were lively and varied. While many congratulated him, he was also subjected to a barrage of insults from neo-Nazi groups particularly active on social networks.

After publication, Kenneth received an endless stream of thank-you messages. His mailbox was literally overflowing. He tried to read every message and, when time allowed, replied to some of them. Among this tide of e-mails, an intriguing message had crept in. It came from a disposable address, tarakna1984@yopmail.com, and bore an enigmatic title: "You forgot something...".

Kenneth had skimmed through the message before relegating it to the archives. He had decided not to delete it permanently, a caution dictated by instinctive hesitation. You never know...

Chapter 10

Kenneth rose at the crack of dawn, ready to face another intense day. As soon as he arrived at the firm, one client followed another without respite, each bringing his own set of concerns and requests. Kenneth, a seasoned but exhausted lawyer, was looking forward to his well-deserved break. Another appointment, he thought, as he made his way to the waiting room.

- Good morning, sir.

- Hello Mr. Lewis.

- Please, come in.

Tarakna, who had taken care to conceal his true identity when making the appointment, entered the office with calculated curiosity. His eyes scanned every nook and cranny, assessing the security features. Once seated, he watched as Kenneth tapped away at his keyboard, meticulously analyzing his surroundings.

- Sir, your firm is packed with cutting-edge technologies. You seem to be a true enthusiast.

- Let's just say I try to stay at the cutting edge so as not to be left behind.

- In my opinion, you're ahead of the game. There are cameras everywhere and even facial recognition to unlock the front door. It's really impressive.

- It really does make my life easier and prevents me from losing my keys, which used to happen a lot. I had to go home dozens of times to get them, leaving my customers to wait... It's much more practical this way.

- I totally understand.

- As for the cameras, especially in the waiting room, they enable me to monitor arrivals without having to move. The only drawback is that the video server is a little noisy. For the rest, it's perfect.

Kenneth was clearly enjoying this conversation. For him, any opportunity to break the monotony was welcome. Tarakna, sensing this, went on.

- But a little walking is good for you. Sitting around all day isn't ideal. Is it?

- Oh, if you only knew the number of steps I take between my desk and the photocopier! Some files force me to go back and forth incessantly. By the end of the day, I'm exhausted - my legs just won't carry me!

- I can see that. I didn't imagine it like that.

Tarakna took in all the details of the cabinet layout. His inner excitement was growing. Everything was going perfectly, every element falling into place. "Soon it won't just be your legs that will fail you," he thought silently, staring at the lawyer with a disturbing intensity.

At the evening, as agreed with the lawyer, Tarakna e-mailed the necessary documents for a fictitious legal proceeding, carefully designed to conceal his true purpose. Nestled in the attachment was a computer bomb, ready to explode.

The second Kenneth clicked on the file, a sophisticated program discreetly installed itself, escaping the vigilance of the antivirus. His phone, plugged into the computer and charging, was also infected. The lawyer's every move on the mobile device would now not escape Tarakna's eye.

The first consequence of the infection was that Kenneth's schedule was immediately turned upside down. The second customer of the following day, initially scheduled for 9.30 a.m., was postponed until 10 a.m. An automatic SMS informed him of this. A slight change, but one with far-reaching consequences...

Chapter 11

Kenneth gently closed the heavy leather-bound volume. His book, finally published, represented the culmination of two years' hard work. Yet this long-awaited triumph was accompanied by a yawning emptiness he couldn't fill. Writing, once his haven, was now giving way to an insidious and implacable solitude, pushing him inexorably towards the meanders of the Web, the Internet.

Every evening, as soon as he got home, he'd sit in front of his computer, eyes glued to the screen. The hours ticked away as he lost himself in the hypnotic scrolling of social networks, that window onto a fake world. Kenneth occasionally tried to make contact with single women, but his efforts were in vain, as ephemeral as a waking dream. Distance, differences in character, nagging memories of his ex-wife, all contributed to the failure of his attempts.

The days went by like copies of the same monotonous pattern. He had tried to dive back into his legal files in the evenings, hoping to find an escape, but the exercise left him drained, unable to discern the beginning and end of his days. This weariness invaded him, gradually eroding his willpower.

Resigned, Kenneth took refuge once again in the virtual world of social networks, US TV series and dating apps. This insidious routine even infiltrated his work time. He no longer hesitated to pull out his phone in the office, eager for new notifications and unread posts. A pernicious addiction to screens had set in, making any attempt to disconnect almost impossible.

The divorce had driven his daughter away, a death blow that had plunged him into a deep depression. Kenneth, feeling the ground beneath his feet, decided to consult a psychologist. The doctor prescribed antidepressants and suggested a detox stay - a modern solution for the troubled soul. Kenneth accepted the suggestion with a sigh of relief. His refuge would be Greece, more specifically the enchanting island of Crete, a place that perhaps promised a rebirth, a new lease of life to his gloomy existence.

Chapter 12

Building Asklepios had given Tarakna unrivalled expertise. He now mastered every stage of the process, from meticulous data collection to sophisticated training of the artificial intelligence. His tests had enabled him to distinguish crucial from superfluous data, thus optimizing the performance of the clones in comparison with their originals. This ability to precisely target essential data opened up promising prospects.

Tarakna was planning to launch a start-up based on this innovative concept. He planned to offer interested parties the opportunity to provide the data needed to guarantee a form of immortality by creating their own digital clone. Through a process of continuous exchange with their double, individuals would be able to refine and improve their clone's behavior by evaluating its actions, good or bad, in the same way Tarakna had done with the subjects of his experiments. But for the moment, his mind was elsewhere.

Originally, Tarakna had undertaken this ambitious quest to create a clone of his late father. The prodigious results obtained with Asklepios had confirmed the viability of his project. However, just as he was about to embark on this adventure, an unexpected newspaper article he stumbled across upset his plans:

Tennis legend Andre Agassi learned how to beat his rival Becker by observing his tongue.

Legendary American tennis player Andre Agassi lost his first three matches against Boris Becker. Then he realized that Becker was hinting at his serves with a little tic.

In a 2017 interview with The Players Tribune's Unscripted, Agassi said he struggled to return Becker's serve. Then, after studying film, he noticed that Becker indicated how he was going to serve by moving his tongue.

"I started to realize he had this weird tic with his tongue," Agassi said. "I'm not kidding. He'd go into his swing, the same routine, and just as he was about to throw the ball, he'd stick his tongue out. And it was either in the middle of his lip, or in the left corner of his lip.

"If Becker served on a tie and put his tongue in the middle of his lip, he served either in the middle or to the body. But if he put it to the side, he was going to serve wide."

Learning this tic helped Agassi turn Becker's serves around, but he had another challenge: not letting Becker know he could guess his serves.

"The hardest part wasn't returning his serve - it was not letting him know I knew that," said Agassi. "I had to resist the temptation to read his serve for the majority of the match and choose the moment when I was going to use that information on a given point to execute a shot that would allow me to turn the match around."

After losing to Becker in their first three matches, Agassi went on to win eight consecutive matches against Becker, including such important victories as the 1990 US Open and French Open semi-finals. He finished with a 10-4 record against Becker, although Becker's fourth win came in the 1995 Wimbledon final.

Agassi said he then revealed the tic to Becker over a beer at Oktoberfest - and Becker was stunned, as he was puzzled as to how Agassi could read it.

"We went out and had a beer together, and I couldn't help but say, 'By the way, did you know you were doing this and revealing your service?'"

"He almost fell out of his chair. He said, 'I used to come home all the time and tell my wife, it's like he's reading my mind.'"

- Scott. Davis

The article reveals with striking acuity that an outside eye can offer us unsuspected insights into ourselves, details we are incapable of perceiving on our own. During speeches, speakers often succumb to the excessive repetition of certain words or expressions, while remaining blind to this verbal tic. This blindness also extends to facial expressions and gestures. It was thanks to this meticulous observation that Agassi was able to anticipate Becker's services, even though the latter was unaware of the reason.

Understanding someone by observing them in minute detail raises a fascinating question: would it be possible to apply this method to better understand oneself, by dialoguing with one's own clone? This was the thought Tarakna had arrived at. Armed with this revelation, he had forged a leitmotif for his personal quest: " *I elevate myself by rising above myself.*" These words, echoing loudly in his head, reflected his determination to perfect himself on his own terms, by rising above his own limitations.

Chapter 13

It was a routine day, or almost. Kenneth left his home, ready to start a new day at his practice. The rising sun bathed the street in a golden glow as he climbed into his car. But no sooner had he started up than a shrill creak was heard from beneath the vehicle. He slammed on the brakes, heart pounding, and got out to inspect the source of the noise.

Indeed, the passenger tire was completely flat. Kenneth gritted his teeth, his nine o'clock appointment with his first customer of the day already looking compromised. "She'll wait," he thought, annoyance marking his face. Hesitating to call a breakdown mechanic, he finally decided to change the wheel himself, although he wasn't looking forward to getting his hands dirty.

It had been a long time since he'd done this kind of work. His rims, without hubcaps, were fitted with chrome studs that hid the nuts. He had to remove them one by one with dedicated tweezers, a tedious task that didn't amuse him. Kenneth wasn't a do-it-yourself kind of guy.

With the spare wheel finally in place, Kenneth went home to wash his hands. The wipes in the glove compartment hadn't been enough to remove the black grime embedded in his skin. He couldn't appear like this in front of his customers, but time was of the essence. His client must have been waiting for him for some time.

He sped off towards the office. What he didn't know was that a *tracking* device, a GPS chip, had been discreetly installed under the left fender of his car. From then on, his every move was monitored. And in his office, a very strange case was unfolding, ready to upset the course of his routine day.

Chapter 14

Kenneth, or at least a man who looked strangely like him, stood in front of the cabinet door. The door unlocked automatically. The facial recognition had worked perfectly. He was dragging a bulky suitcase behind him, which he hoisted with effort before pushing the door open with his shoulder.

Moments later, the first customer of the day appeared. She glanced at the clock in the waiting room: 8:50. She was a little early, precisely ten minutes before her appointment. Grabbing the first magazine from the stack on the coffee table, she settled down to wait, absent-mindedly flipping through the pages.

Less than a minute later, the lawyer opened his office door and walked towards her. She felt a sense of satisfaction at having arrived early. Perhaps she'd leave earlier, she thought, unaware of what lay ahead.

- Hello, Mrs. Oliveira. How are you? asked the lawyer with a professional smile.

- Hello, Mr. Lewis. I'm fine, thank you. How are you?

- Very well, thank you. Please follow me.

He closed the door behind him and walked towards her as she was about to sit down on the chair in front of his desk. His hand came to rest on her shoulder, causing her to turn in surprise. Before she knew what was happening, the lawyer's lips were already moving away from hers. He'd just stolen a kiss.

Furious, she pushed him away and, in a fit of rage, grabbed a vase from the desk and threw it in his face. The assailant's blood ran cold. He shoved her violently, and her head hit a radiator with a thud. She collapsed, inert. The shock had been unbelievably violent. She died instantly.

The lawyer, in a panic, began to walk in circles. He had clearly not foreseen this turn of events. The firm's video surveillance camera was capturing everything. Panicking, he dragged the body to a corner of the office, away from the door, then headed for the CCTV management PC. Inserting a USB key, which first flashed red, he waited a few seconds. The key turned green. The video recording of the entire scene, approximately ten minutes, was sucked into the key before being erased from the machine. The recording in progress was suspended, just long enough for him to leave the premises. A malicious program, a malware, was implanted in the system, enabling remote access at will. A crucial piece of evidence was removed and the machine corrupted. The machine's password was also changed.

He picked up his suitcase and left the office as if nothing had happened. A few seconds later, the video surveillance system resumed normal operation, exactly as programmed by the malware.

Chapter 15

Kenneth finally arrived at his office some thirty minutes late. As usual, the door unlocked automatically, and he headed for his office. A strange feeling suddenly came over him. He turned to look around. His face flushed with astonishment as he discovered the macabre scene before him. A young woman, decapitated and covered in blood, lay on the ground. Her lifeless body lay there, in his own office, and he had no idea what had happened.

Trembling and distraught, Kenneth grabbed his phone to call the police. But before he could reach his pocket, the door to his study was smashed in with a deafening crash. Instinctively, he covered his head and crouched at the foot of the wall to protect himself. A dozen police officers burst in:

- Raise your hands and don't move!

Someone had obviously been quicker than Kenneth to notify the police...

Chapter 16

It was now three hours since Dihya's plane had left Paris. Soon, it would begin its descent. Apart from a few weeks during the summer season, there were no direct flights from Paris to Chania, Crete, forcing a connection in Athens. For Dihya, this detour was not a constraint, but a blessing. She was always enchanted by the splendor of the Greek capital. And now Athens loomed on the horizon, the landing imminent. Dihya pressed her face against the window, determined to capture every fragment of the spectacle before her.

From the skies above, Athens was revealed as a dazzling jewel set against a sea of azure. The soft green hills undulated gently around the city, and in the center, like an eternal diadem, the Acropolis stood proudly.

With her heart pounding, Dihya let herself be enchanted by the majesty of the scene. The Parthenon stood with timeless grandeur, its white marble columns cut with almost supernatural purity against the deep blue of the Greek sky. The sun's rays caressed the ancient stones, revealing shades of gold and ochre, while delicate shadows danced among the ruins, whispering tales of ancient gods and heroes.

Below, the modern city spread out like a mosaic of red roofs and busy streets, offering a vibrant contrast to the solemn serenity of the Acropolis. Olive and cypress trees, like silent guardians, encircled the sacred temples, adding a touch of greenery to this epic tableau. Dihya thought of the countless stories she had read and studied, the tales of philosophers and warriors who had trodden this sacred soil.

The Theater of Dionysus loomed in a semicircle at the foot of the hill, its stone tiers still waiting to hear the echoes of tragedies and comedies that had once inflamed the passions of ancient spectators. Dihya imagined those spectators of yesteryear, vibrating with emotion at every act, every scene. She even imagined her ancestors applauding their brothers at athletic competitions.

Athens, seen from the sky, was more than just a city; it was an eternal poem etched in stone, a sanctuary of the past where the spirits of the ancient gods still seemed to roam, imbuing the air with an almost tangible presence. Dihya, on the plane, felt this deep connection with history and time, an irresistible call to explore and tell the stories that formed the fabric of humanity.

The plane is airtight, but at the mere mention of certain memories in her mind, Dihya could almost feel the wind bringing with it the scent of orange trees and the murmur of the Aegean Sea. A true journey within a journey.

As the plane drew closer to the ground, leaving only the austere surroundings of the airport visible through the window, a certain melancholy seized Dihya. Time had flown by without her realizing it, and already she was wandering through the stores in the departure hall. She had to be patient before setting off again for Chania. Her footsteps echoed lightly on the polished marble floor. With her backpack slung tightly over her shoulders, she observed with lively curiosity the colorful, bustling displays around her. Her blue eyes, sparkling with intelligence and passion, scanned the memorabilia and items on display, each seeming to tell a unique story. Her wavy blond hair, slightly tousled from travel, framed her face marked by the enthusiasm of exploration. She wore a light beige linen shirt, ideal for warm climates, and practical cargo pants, revealing her taste for adventure and comfort.

Dihya lingered in front of a newsstand, leafing through the pages of local and international magazines. She stopped in front of an artisanal jewelry stand, admiring the silver bracelets and pendants adorned with blue stones reminiscent of the colors of the Aegean Sea. Her fingers delicately brushed the pearls and gems, appreciating the meticulous workmanship of Greek artisans. Her silver earrings, adorned with coral, reminded her of the deep and ancient links between Mediterranean cultures.

Continuing her wanderings, Dihya headed for a bookshop, her eyes lighting up at the sight of rows of books with attractive covers. She ran her fingers along the edges of the books, reading the titles with interest. She finally chose a book on the island of Delos, hoping to deepen her knowledge of this mythologically resonant piece of land, and much more besides for her.

As she left the bookshop, she spotted a café where she decided to sit for a while. Ordering a Greek coffee and a pastry, she sat down at a table by the window, watching the bustle of the airport as she immersed herself in her reading. With every page she turned, Dihya felt more and more connected to the history of this ancient land, her mind whirling between the present and the echoes of the past. Time seemed to stand still as she savored this moment of tranquility and discovery, waiting for her flight to Chania, Crete.

Chapter 17

Tarakna removed his wig and mask. The oppressive air of the room suddenly seemed less heavy. Heaving a sigh of relief, he took the USB key out of his pocket and watched the recording of the crime scene. His face, very similar to the lawyer's, had been enough to fool the naive client. However, his body, far from Kenneth's athletic figure, would not stand up to the scrutiny of the police. He therefore had to resort to subtle digital retouching to alter the video. Off to the airport to catch a plane to his bunker and get to work.

In the course of extracting data from Kenneth's computer, Tarakna had come across a gold mine: the history of the surveillance cameras. These recordings, offering images of the lawyer from every angle and for long sequences, were a godsend for a data manipulation expert like him. A few minutes' processing would be enough to extract the scenes useful for training an AI capable of transferring the lawyer's morphology onto any other video. This is the principle of *swapping*, which involves replacing one person with another in an image or video using sophisticated AI-based algorithms. Tarakna applied this process to the crime scene, substituting his own silhouette with that of the lawyer.

Thanks to his remote access to the law firm's server, Tarakna had been able to retrieve the video of Kenneth's arrival at the law firm, just before he discovered the victim's body. This video provided invaluable details of the lawyer's exact attire on the day of the crime, ensuring a perfect *swap of* both body and clothing. The result was breathtaking, a true masterpiece, a *deepfake** indistinguishable from the rest of the recording. All that remained was to insert this modified video into the surveillance camera feed.

Tarakna quickly executed. Connecting to the server, he transferred the deepfake and read back the recording, starting a few seconds before the moment of insertion. He wanted to make sure that everything worked perfectly. The transition was impeccable, so much so that even he couldn't distinguish where the *deepfake* began.

It wouldn't be long before the police would seize the server for investigation, and Kenneth would find himself in an awkward position. The password he provided would not work, making his situation even worse. For the investigators, this apparent refusal to cooperate would mean he had something to hide. Tarakna's plan was meticulously elaborated, every detail carefully thought out. A veritable web where every thread was in its place, nothing left to chance...

---

* The term deepfake comes from the contraction of the words "deep learning" and "fake". It refers to a digital manipulation technique using AI to create falsified images, videos or audios, capable of convincingly imitating the appearance, voice or actions of a real person. In the context of this book, the concept of deepfake is broadened to also include the falsification of historical facts and *deeply* held beliefs, but without any real foundation.

Chapter 18

Through the plane's window, Dihya admired a picturesque beauty. First, she saw splinters of islets and islands scattered across the azure immensity of the Aegean Sea, like precious pearls scattered across an infinite blue fabric. These small land masses emerged from the crystal-clear waters, each offering a unique spectacle. Some islands were simple rocky outcrops, almost bare, with only a few green dots, barely visible from the sky. Others, a little larger, were adorned with denser vegetation, silver olive trees and maritime pines whose dark green needles contrasted with the brilliant blue of the sea. Beaches of fine sand or polished pebbles lined these islands, and Dihya spotted tiny isolated coves, inaccessible other than by boat, where the water took on hues of turquoise and jade. Small white houses with blue roofs, typical of Cycladic architecture, appeared here and there, often grouped together in picturesque hamlets. Orthodox churches, with their blue domes and whitewashed walls, stood proudly on some of these islands, adding a touch of spiritual serenity to the landscape. Continuing to gaze, Dihya noticed a few larger islands, covered in terraced crops, with vineyards and fields of golden wheat stretching out in a patchwork pattern. Tiny harbors, where colorful fishing boats floated lazily, added a touch of life to these serene islands.

Gradually, as the plane moved forward, the island of Crete began to take shape on the horizon. At first a dark line on the horizon, it gradually became an imposing landmass, its majestic mountains standing like sentinels. The vegetation grew lusher, the hills were adorned with dense forests and cultivated fields, and the coasts revealed golden beaches and steep cliffs plunging into the sea.

Dihya felt her excitement rise at the sight of Crete, an island steeped in history and myth, whose imposing silhouette was taking shape with increasing clarity. As the plane began its descent, the details of the Cretan land became sharper.

Chapter 19

Kenneth was brutally dragged away by the police, his body thrown into the cage of a van that sped down the Parisian streets, siren blaring. He kept pinching himself, struggling to believe that he wasn't dreaming, or rather, that he wasn't living a nightmare from which he desperately yearned to wake up. Alas, harsh reality was upon him. Here he was, being treated like a criminal, just days before defending a family against the same heinous accusations he was now facing. A strange role reversal indeed.

Behind bars, his cries of innocence and desperate explanations were met with indifference from the agents. They remained unmoved, letting him flounder like a trapped animal, without the slightest chance to explain himself. Deep down, Kenneth knew that his protests were futile, that nothing could magically set him free. But the instinct to survive drove him to try the impossible to escape this infernal trap.

When he arrived at the 17^e arrondissement police station, he was ruthlessly thrown into a filthy cell. The walls bore the scars of repulsive filth, and traces of excrement and urine poisoned the air. Kenneth tried to hold his breath, to cover his nose with his shirt, but the stench seeped everywhere, making him sick.

After two hours of unbearable waiting, he was finally led to a telephone. Confident of his innocence, he called an influential friend at the Home Office, a politician who owed him a favor. He'd managed to get him off a serious charge of sexual harassment and rape, and Kenneth now hoped this friend could return the favor. He also contacted a famous lawyer, Mr.

Hanfman, counting on his expertise to get him out of this desperate situation.

Eight long hours of interrogation later, Kenneth was released on parole. He breathed a sigh of relief, although the threat of a legal battle still hung over him. The victim's family had not yet come forward, but he knew this respite would be short-lived. He'd seen many miscarriages of justice, and the prospect of months of anguish and uncertainty frightened him.

There was still a glimmer of hope, however. Kenneth had not been banned from leaving the country, which meant that his digital detox trip to Greece could go ahead. This trip would be a welcome breath of fresh air, a temporary escape from the misfortune that had befallen him. Already packing his bags, he prepared to leave, seeking a semblance of peace away from this Parisian nightmare.

Chapter 20

Dihya finally caught sight of Chania, revealing itself with enchanting beauty. The green hills sloped gently down to the turquoise sea, where waves lapped the golden sandy beaches. The town itself, a harmonious blend of historic and modern buildings, stretched along the coast.

As the plane drew closer, Dihya could see Souda Bay, a deep-blue jewel-box bordered by majestic mountains. Nestling in the heart of this bay, the NATO naval base stretched out, its orderly facilities contrasting with the surrounding natural landscape. Docks and military buildings were visible, testifying to the strategic importance of this location. The base was the largest and most important U.S. and NATO base in the eastern Mediterranean. What's more, it was the only deep-water port in southern Europe suitable and capable of accommodating the largest vessels. Dihya's gaze was drawn to the imposing presence of the American aircraft carrier USS Harry S. Truman, which dominated the scene. This immense ship, a floating fortress, was anchored in the bay, surrounded by several other smaller warships. The carrier's decks were bustling with activity, fighter planes lined up like sentinels ready to launch into the skies. The contrast between the military might of the base and the serenity of the surrounding nature was striking. The verdant mountains seemed to silently watch over the bay, their peaks bathed in golden light, while the calm waters reflected the blue sky and the silhouettes of the ships.

Dihya, fascinated by the view, pondered the complex history of Crete, an island that had always been a strategic crossroads in the Mediterranean. She thought of the ancient civilizations that had flourished here, the epic naval battles, and the modern wars that had also left their mark.

As the plane began its descent towards Chania airport, Dihya spotted numerous military aircraft parked not far from the runway. Khaki green barracks were also visible a few steps away. This was clearly a place where the boundary between civilian and military was thin, if not non-existent. Dihya felt a mixture of excitement and respect for this quiet place, whose decor was reminiscent of the ever-present sound of boots. Whatever the case, the panoramic view of the bay hosting the USS Harry S. Truman would undoubtedly remain etched in her memory, a powerful symbol of the many stories this land and its waters had to offer.

Chapter 21

Tarakna activated an instance of Asklepios built in his image with his own personal data. Each time this digital clone started up, the screen lit up with the same message: *"I'm elevating myself by rising above myself."*

For Tarakna, interacting with Asklepios had become a habit, a kind of intellectual game. He could spend hours conversing with his digital double, discovering unconscious tics, but also flaws in his ability to explain complex concepts simply. This practice had in fact revealed a disarming truth: he suffered from the "curse of the expert", a plague that prevents scientists from effectively popularizing their knowledge when addressing a lay audience.

Tarakna had taken care to create a rigorous framework for the experiments that had enabled him to discover this. He never addressed Asklepios by his own name. He called himself *Tissist*, thus avoiding confusion and respecting the law of the excluded third, according to which a proposition cannot be both true and false. To imagine Tarakna explaining a concept to Tarakna would have been a paradox.

To avoid bias, he avoided asking questions on subjects he had mastered. If his clone provided explanations, he would understand them too easily, making it impossible to assess clarity. Instead, Tarakna would turn to areas he knew less about, providing his clone with preliminary resources, such as documents or links to websites. Asklepios' answers were often convoluted, far from clear. To ensure that the problem wasn't with the AI itself, he would ask the same questions of other Asklepios clones, receiving clearer answers. Only his clone was suffering from this malady, just like himself.

This rigorous method had enabled Tarakna to discover aspects of himself he'd never known existed. Each new revelation invariably brought him back to the same thought:

"I elevate myself by rising above myself."

Chapter 22

Dihya collected her luggage and hurried across the small Chania Airport towards the exit to catch a cab. After waiting a few minutes among the passengers, a female cab driver beckoned. Dihya pushed her luggage-laden cart towards the car. The driver helped her put the luggage in the trunk, politely refusing any help from Dihya.

- Where are you going, ma'am?

- To Stratos Villas, Melidhónion, please.

- Do you have the exact address?

Dihya handed her phone to the driver, who glanced at it before entering the destination into the GPS. The route appeared instantly on the car's screen.

- We'll be there in three quarters of an hour, 43 minutes to be exact, announced the lady cabbie. There's a bottle of water at your disposal, right next to your feet, if you get thirsty.

Dihya, although not really thirsty, thought a sip of water would be welcome. She grabbed the bottle and took a few sips.

The road was pleasant, and the driver generously shared information on places to visit and dishes to enjoy, as Greek cabs often do, well aware of the importance of tourism for their country. However, one question nagged at Dihya. Every street in the city was lined with orange trees, overflowing with mouth-watering oranges, yet nobody seemed to be enjoying them. She finally asked.

- Could you tell me why there are all these orange trees on the sidewalks and nobody's taking advantage of them?

- You're not the first to ask this question. Orange trees are found in many Mediterranean regions, including Seville for example.

These oranges are extremely bitter and inedible as they are. They are used to make marmalades and cosmetics. Their flowers are used to make perfumes. Moreover, these trees flourish here without much water and play a decorative role while reducing pollution. And that's why!

- Thanks to you, I'll be able to sleep a lot easier tonight!

The city quickly disappeared in the rearview mirror, giving way to the bay of Souda stretching out below. The driver negotiated the winding bends with almost supernatural ease, reminiscent of a Formula 1 driver in perfect symbiosis with his vehicle. Dihya, in admiration, thought of her own life. She had changed careers out of passion, seeking that same harmony.

- We're almost there. See the four villas over there?

- Yes, I recognize them.

Dihya had done some research on the Internet before coming. The unique configuration of this residence, nestled in the heart of an olive grove, was easily recognizable. Four small, fortress-like stone villas with vast terraces offering panoramic views. Surrounded by lawn, intersected by paved driveways and a large, round swimming pool, like a giant blue eye.

The car turned off the main road onto a narrow lane. A large wooden gate, bearing the name STRATOS VILLAS in large white letters, stood in front of them.

- Here we are, smiles the driver. Didn't you get dizzy with the turns?

- A little, but it'll do.

The driver set down Dihya's suitcases and handed her business card.

- If you need a cab for the return journey or to go somewhere, just give me a call. Enjoy your stay.

Dihya thanked the woman before rethinking the word "stay" she had just heard. Hers was a particular one, an attempt to free herself from addiction to screens and social networks, that explosive cocktail that forms the digital heroine. A holiday, yes, but above all a quest to regain a certain freedom.

Dihya rang the gate bell and announced her arrival over the intercom. The gate opened, revealing an enchanting place. A smile lit up her face. All that remained was to see if the detox program would live up to her expectations...

Chapter 23

Tarakna advanced methodically, each step of his plan meticulously designed to entrap his target, Kenneth. The art of manipulation and deception was his new field of predilection, and this time he intended to use one of the most devious techniques of modern times: *catfishing*. Tarakna had prepared everything to draw Kenneth into a false relationship, nourished by lies and false promises, until the moment when he would brutally reveal the truth, shattering his spirit.

With the rise of social networking and online dating, human relationships had changed profoundly. These technological innovations, while fascinating, had also opened the door to malicious practices such as catfishing. This term describes the creation of a false online identity with the aim of deceiving a victim, often to maintain a fictitious love relationship or to defraud them. The term originates from a documentary called "Catfish", released in 2010, in which Nev Schulman, an American producer, falls in love with a 19-year-old woman who turns out to be a 40-year-old housewife. The film's title was inspired by a technique supposedly used by fishermen who transported cod from Alaska to China. The fish, which had become inert during the long journey, arrived in poor condition. To keep them active, the fishermen added catfish among the cod, forcing them to move to keep them fresh. This anecdote illustrates the concept of catfishing, where an impostor infiltrates his victim's life, manipulating her relentlessly.

Tarakna, thanks to Asklepios, had succeeded in creating perfect clones and intended to exploit this technology to carry out sophisticated catfishing. Kenneth, already weakened, would be easy prey. To this end, Tarakna contacted several attractive women via a dating site, offering them a reward of $10,000 in exchange for their complete personal data. Several accepted. He chose the most beautiful among them. The clone of this chosen one would be called Eurydice.

Waiting for the right moment to act, Tarakna kept a close eye on Kenneth's activities on his devices. Yet something wasn't right: Kenneth's phone was strangely silent. No calls, no text messages, nothing. Kenneth, usually addicted to his mobile and social networks, seemed to have disappeared off the radar. This silence worried Tarakna, making his fear that the malware installed on Kenneth's phone had failed. While this didn't totally compromise his plan, it did deprive Tarakna of a strategic advantage.

Just as he was about to leave his bunker for a walk, a ringtone sounded. He pulled his phone out of his pocket, his heart pounding. An outgoing call from Kenneth. Tarakna breathed a sigh of relief, but curiosity consumed him. Who was Kenneth calling on this unusual number, and why now?

After a few seconds of ringing, a voice answered the other end of the line. Tarakna didn't miss a word of the conversation, his phone practically glued to his ear.

- Hi, Mom.

- Hello, Kenneth, how are you dear son? It's been a long time.

- Yes, I know, I know. I'm sorry about that. I've been very busy, especially writing the book, as you know.

- It doesn't matter, my son. The main thing is that you're well. Congratulations on your book. I'm so proud of you.

- Thanks, Mum. I was also calling to let you know I'll be by to see you tomorrow.

- Tell me it's not true. I'm so glad. I'll be waiting for you impatiently.

Tarakna frowned, puzzled. What was Kenneth doing in Scotland? Was he planning to escape French justice? Whatever the case, he'd be on his tail wherever he went. He wouldn't let go of his prey.

Chapter 24

Kenneth was looking forward to returning to the town of his childhood. In these troubled times, the place that embodies security is often the place where you grew up. After an hour and forty-minute flight from Paris CDG, he finally arrived at Edinburgh airport.

Sitting in the cab on his way to his parents' home in Bridge of Allan, near Stirling, Kenneth relived in his mind's eye the most precious memories of his youth. Nostalgia washed over him as the familiar landscapes flashed before his eyes.

Bridge of Allan is a picturesque town in central Scotland, renowned for its charming atmosphere, historic architecture and natural beauty. The town's close-knit community comes alive every year at the Strathallan Games, one of the region's most eagerly awaited events, a traditional Highland gathering. The games celebrate Scottish culture through a variety of disciplines, attracting young and old in a whirlwind of festivities. Competitions include athletics, thrilling races and throwing events, as well as Highland dancing contests. Bagpipe and drum competitions, echoing across the valley, are highlights of the celebration. Heavy sports, such as log throwing and hammer throwing, demonstrate the strength and endurance of the participants, recalling the ancestral traditions of the Highlands. Children, meanwhile, take part in age-appropriate games such as foot races and tug-of-war competitions, contributing to the festive atmosphere and the transmission of Scottish traditions. These activities not only entertain, but also instill a sense of pride and cultural heritage in the younger generation.

For Kenneth, every street corner, every house, every tree in Bridge of Allan evoked memories of a past that was long gone, but still alive within him. His return to this town was not simply a journey through space, but a true pilgrimage to the heart of his roots, where every stone, every breath of wind told a story of courage, tradition and belonging.

Kenneth remembered it all, and the sound of the bagpipes was still ringing in his ears. He was lost in thought when the cab driver interrupted him:

- Here we are!

Kenneth saw his parents' house rise up before his eyes. A lightning-fast plunge into the past. Nothing had changed in the house where he had spent his childhood. It had retained all its originality in every detail, compared to what he had always known. In fact, the houses in this picturesque little town all looked alike. Combining traditional Scottish and Victorian styles, they were built of local stone. They featured stone facades, slate roofs, sash windows and ornamental details in wood or iron. Decorative elements included cornices, pediments and dormer windows, with well-kept gardens surrounded by fences or hedges. Sloping roofs and elaborate chimneys completed the town's traditional charm.

Kenneth got out of the cab and collected his luggage. He didn't go straight to his mother's house. He took a moment to look around, to contemplate the neighborhood in which he had grown up. He spotted the Westerton Arms, a traditional restaurant run by neighbors for generations. The tall, handsome clock on a large wrought-iron post in front of the establishment was also still there. Kenneth smiled happily as he saw the restaurant door open and people coming out. It was still alive and well, and it was good to see the family business still going strong, which was also part of the town's charm.

Kenneth took his two large suitcases and pushed open the small door onto the driveway. He rang the doorbell. A moment later, his mother opened the door.

- Hello, son. Welcome home. I've missed you!

- Hello, Mom, thank you. I missed you too.

Kenneth's mother was astonished to see her son loaded like a mule. What was going on? Had he abandoned his life in France to come back here? She was worried and wanted to know a little more.

- Are you moving or what with your big suitcases?

- Ah, it's a long story.

- What do you mean, a long story? Are you definitely coming back here? Did you lose your job?

- No, Mom, don't worry. I'm not moving back in.

- It's not that you're coming back here that worries me so much, but...

Kenneth stopped her in her tracks, trying to keep her from fretting and stressing, which was the last thing she needed at her age.

- I'm just passing through, Mom. I'm leaving tomorrow morning for a long vacation in Greece. That's why I've packed so much luggage.

As he was packing his suitcases in the corner of the hallway, Kenneth's phone rang. He paused to pick it up. It was an anonymous call.

- Hello, this is the Paris police. Are we speaking with Mr. Kenneth Lewis?

- Hello, that's right, himself.

- As part of our investigation, we have seized your office computer. We will now proceed with the inspection. We have, of course, obtained prior judicial authorization. You're currently abroad, aren't you?

- Yes, I'm staying with my parents in Scotland.

- In order to comply scrupulously with procedure and since you are absent, the officer in charge of the investigation has appointed two witnesses to attend.

- Okay, fine. How can I help you?

- Your computer is password-protected. We need it to unlock it.

- Ah sorry, I thought I'd already given it to you. It's "Magali@1996". Let me spell it out for you:

- Capital "M",
- lowercase "a",
- lowercase "g",
- lowercase "a",

- lowercase "l",
- lowercase "i",
- @, at or arobase,
- 1996

- Thank you, Mr. Lewis. Duly noted. Have a nice day.

Kenneth's sad face called out to his mother:

- What's the matter? Are you in trouble?

- No, it's nothing. It was just my replacement at the office who needed a password to use a machine.

Kenneth didn't want to worry his elderly, heart-sick mother. He preferred to lie to her. The practice had, of course, been closed since his sad affair.

- Was that the name "Magali" I just heard?" asked his mother, curious. It sounds like you still care about her.

- No, not really. We split up and she's moved on. I just need to take the time to bring it all up to date. I have to think about it too.

- No matter what you tell me, I'll never understand why it was you who left to continue your studies in France and not her who stayed here in Scotland after you met at Glasgow University. You have the heart of a sweetheart, my darling.

- Mom, please, forget it. It's in the past. Well, I'll finish packing and come in for tea.

Kenneth returned to his childhood home, and his mother had lost none of her habits. She pampered him like a little child. She served him his favorite traditional cake, a Selkirk Bannock she'd baked that morning especially for him, accompanied by a cup of hot tea. He was ecstatic.

After a long discussion about the world, their world, his mother handed him a letter.

- Here, I just got this this morning. I don't know why it was sent here.

Kenneth was astonished. He didn't live there anymore, and there was no reason why someone should send him a letter to that address. He promptly opened it, unfolded the letter and looked at what it said:

"I follow you everywhere. You forgot something."

At the bottom of the letter was an enigmatic signature:

- TARAKNA -

Chapter 25

Kenneth had the strange impression of having read or heard this sentence somewhere before: "You've forgotten something". Try as he might, he couldn't remember where. He remained pensive for a moment, trying to reassure himself that it was simply a joke. With some resignation, he took a photo of the letter with his phone before throwing it into the fireplace. No need to bother with that, he thought.

Night was falling, and dinnertime was approaching. His mother had prepared a meal that promised to delight him: haggis, an emblematic dish of Scottish cuisine that he hadn't tasted in years, unable to find it in France. Haggis, a sheep's belly stuffed with a mixture of mutton liver, heart and lungs, onions, oatmeal, suet and spices, evoked warm memories of past family meals.

The evening passed quickly, and Kenneth, exhausted by his journey, promptly fell asleep. He knew he'd have to get up early the next morning to begin the next leg of his journey, a longer one with an inevitable stopover.

After a long embrace with his mother, he took a cab to Edinburgh airport. Four hours later, he arrived in Athens. As he paced the boarding hall, looking for a bench to sit and consult his ticket, an announcement drew him from his thoughts:

- Mr. Kenneth Lewis is expected at gate 23 for immediate boarding of flight AEE 6254 to Chania. This is the last call.

Kenneth quickened his pace, his mind oscillating between the urgency of the situation and a latent anxiety that never seemed to leave him. Kenneth had thought he had a comfortable margin between his two flights, but he had been sorely mistaken. A slight delay to the first flight had upset his plans, forcing him into a frantic race not to miss his flight to Crete. He had barely set foot in the aircraft when the door closed behind him. The plane was just waiting for him to take off.

The flight was short, barely an hour to reach the largest Greek island from the mainland. Half an hour by cab later, Kenneth finally arrived at his accommodation. Casa Delfino, family-owned for six generations, is a charming hotel nestled in a 17th-century Venetian mansion in the heart of Chania's old walled town. Crossing the threshold into the reception area, Kenneth entered a courtyard paved with pebbles, adorned with several trees, including a majestic palm, and adorned at its center with a large pot overflowing with luxuriant branches. Tables were laid out, offering a romantic haven of peace, ideal for dining, reading or simply relaxing. Kenneth was pleased with his choice of hotel. In the morning or evening, he could enjoy a rooftop terrace, high enough to offer a panoramic view of the surrounding area, including the harbor dominated by its lighthouse, just a few steps away.

For the moment, he was obsessed with a single thought: taking a good shower and going to bed. As he turned off the lights, he suddenly remembered that he had to call his mother to let her know he'd arrived safely. The scene reminded him of all those nights in his childhood when his mother would come and turn off the light in his room once he was asleep. The stay at Bridge of Allan had obviously revived old memories. He picked up his phone:

- Siri, call my mother.

Kenneth's command split the air of the small, deserted apartment. He expected to hear his mother's gentle voice, but instead the mechanical tone of the telephone avatar answered, cold and implacable:

- Your connection is disabled. You cannot make calls except for emergencies.

It was like a brutal reminder of why he was here. Kenneth's face hardened, suddenly realizing he was cut off from the world. He could receive calls, but not make them. The thought that he hadn't informed his mother of this particular constraint flashed through him like a bolt of guilt. Resigned, he typed a succinct message:

Hi Mom, I arrived safely.

Putting the phone down, he fell back onto the bed, exhausted. He closed his eyes, hoping for a respite in the darkness of his closed eyelids, and above all, to fall asleep quickly. Instinctively, his hand reached for his phone again, despite the absence of Internet. A mechanical gesture, a deeply ingrained habit. The need for connection, however virtual, drove him to explore what he could still reach on his device: the photo album.

A recent image, the last one he'd taken, flashed into Kenneth's mind with brilliant intensity, a light so white and dazzling that it literally flooded his room. The words emerged from the screen like an obvious threat:

> *"I follow you everywhere. You forgot something.*
>
> *- TARAKNA -*

An icy shiver ran down his spine, and a dull, almost primal anguish seized him. With a feverish gesture, Kenneth switched off his phone, the screen plunging into a reassuring darkness. He closed his eyes again, trying desperately to banish the image from his mind, to regain his composure and sink quickly into sleep.

Chapter 26

The tour operator responsible for organizing this detox stay had carefully prepared a series of activities for its clients. The first was a long hike through the wilderness, a real challenge for the participants. A bus had been chartered to collect them from their accommodation in Chania and take them to the Omalos plateau.

In the first light of dawn, the coach climbed the winding mountain roads, finally depositing its passengers at the trailhead. The sun was just beginning to peek over the horizon, and the air, still fresh, promised perfect conditions for starting the sixteen-kilometer walk through the Samaria Gorge.

A group of ten people stood ready to venture into this natural sanctuary. Among them were several company executives, more familiar with meeting rooms than rocky trails, who set off with palpable excitement. The first few kilometers were marked by steep descents and slippery rocks, turning their initial enthusiasm into a serious battle against fatigue and the inhospitable terrain.

Halfway along, they stopped for a well-deserved break in the shade of the trees. Faces were flushed with exertion, but conversation was lively. It was at this point that a middle-aged woman in the group began to show more pronounced signs of fatigue. She stumbled slightly over a stone and stood still, trying to catch her breath. Kenneth, athletic and alert, and Dihya, always ready to help, immediately noticed her distress. They approached her to offer their support. Kenneth held out her hand, while Dihya walked beside her, speaking softly to encourage her.

The group resumed their journey at a slower pace, ensuring that no one was left behind. Despite their exhaustion, the executives were beginning to find their rhythm, sharing anecdotes and laughter to lighten the atmosphere. Kenneth and Dihya never took their eyes off their hiking companion, ensuring her stability along the way. Between Kenneth and Dihya, glances met, smiles were born, perhaps a tentative romance was taking root in these wild surroundings.

As they advanced, the scenery revealed itself in all its splendor: towering rock faces, narrow winding passages, crystal-clear rivers. The raw beauty of the gorges captivated every member of the group, despite the difficulties they encountered. The sound of their footsteps on the stones, the song of the birds and the whisper of the wind in the trees composed a spellbinding natural symphony. It's easy to see why the village of Samaria would have been a haven of peace for the region's historic inhabitants, who had been fleeing successive invasions since the dawn of time. Quite simply, this place exudes security and serenity.

After several hours' walking, punctuated by intense efforts and moments of solidarity, the group finally reached the exit of the gorge, near the coastal village of Agia Roumeli. Exhaustion could be seen on their faces, but also immense satisfaction and a sense of camaraderie reinforced by this shared adventure. They headed for the nearby beach, where the cool waters of the Libyan Sea awaited them for a well-deserved swim. Their bus, having taken a long detour by road, was there, ready to take them back, but for the moment, all that mattered were the waves and the victory over themselves they had just won.

Chapter 27

The gentle murmur of the waves washing up on the beach and the dazzling shimmer of the Libyan Sea under the afternoon sun brought a well-deserved respite to all. Tired faces lit up at the thought of a refreshing swim. The group spread out on the warm sand, each finding a place to put down their belongings. Clothes quickly exchanged for swimwear, as impatience took hold of them, each second bringing them closer to the embrace of the crystal-clear waters.

The deep, clear blue sea beckoned irresistibly. Among them, Dihya, a woman of radiant beauty, drew the eye. Her natural grace was revealed when she changed, revealing a figure as graceful as it was sculpted. Her generous bosom could not leave anyone indifferent. Kenneth, an athlete with an imposing but not excessive build, couldn't look away. His broad shoulders and confident smile added to his presence.

Together, they walked towards the sea. The first waves licked their feet, provoking bursts of laughter at the sensation of freshness. They progressed slowly, letting themselves be enveloped by the welcoming waves.

Dihya, with a radiant smile, began to swim with natural ease. Kenneth, meanwhile, cut through the water with impressive speed and endurance. Their aquatic paths soon crossed. Kenneth, noticing Dihya's presence, slowed down, offering a dazzling smile.

- You swim very well, he said, his voice warm with sincerity.

- Thanks, you too, replied Dihya, her eyes shining with mischief. But I think you could easily outrun me.

- Maybe, but it's not a race, Kenneth replied, laughing. I prefer to savor the moment.

They swam side by side, engaging in light, pleasant conversation. The sea, offering a cocoon of tranquility, isolated their exchange from the others. They shared anecdotes, fragments of their lives, discovering common interests.

On the beach, the other members of the group watched them with knowing smiles, noting the obvious chemistry between the two. The sun continued to shine, the waves danced eternally, and Dihya and Kenneth's laughter echoed above the soothing murmur of the sea.

After an invigorating swim, the group gathered on the warm sand, exchanging moments of relaxation and camaraderie. Kenneth sat next to Dihya, handing her a towel. Their conversation continued, each lost in a bubble of complicity despite the presence of the others.

As the day drew to a close, marked by a memorable adventure and strengthened bonds, Dihya and Kenneth felt a promising connivance emerging. The hike through the Samaria Gorge and the swim in the Libyan Sea would remain etched in their memories, bearing witness not only to the challenges they had overcome, but also to the new friendships and unexpected connections they had made.

Chapter 28

After a day full of adventure and discovery, the group prepared to leave Agia Roumeli. They boarded the bus that would take them back to their respective places of residence, tired but filled with memories of hiking and swimming. The bus was comfortable, with cushioned seats and a magnificent view of the Cretan landscape.

Kenneth and Dihya, having shared special moments earlier in the day, naturally chose to sit together. They found two seats near a panoramic window, from which they could watch the countryside go by as the bus moved along.

The bus set off slowly, and a calm atmosphere settled in among the hikers. Some closed their eyes to rest, others chatted in hushed tones, while Kenneth and Dihya continued their conversation, discovering a little more of each other with each passing moment.

- So, tell me, Kenneth, what brought you here to Crete? asked Dihya, her eyes sparkling with curiosity.

Kenneth smiled, looking briefly out the window before answering.

- I'm guessing the same as you, digital detox!

Dihya smiled and nodded.

- On that, we agree. But why Crete?

- Crete seemed the perfect escape, with its beautiful scenery and rich culture, Kenneth replied. Without straying too far from home. And I must say, this hike was exactly what I needed.

- I agree, this island is a beautiful place.

They exchanged stories about their respective lives, past travels and future aspirations. Kenneth spoke of his passion, writing, while Dihya shared her love of investigation and history. Their conversation was fluid, punctuated by laughter and moments of reflection. Kenneth was careful not to talk about his problems and the recent case that had turned his life upside down, for fear of frightening Dihya and perhaps jeopardizing a budding relationship.

At one point, a slight jolt from the bus brought them physically closer. Kenneth instinctively placed his hand on the armrest between them, brushing against Dihya's hand. The contact was brief, but significant, triggering a shy smile from Dihya. Kenneth withdrew his hand with a slight smile, sensing an obvious connection between them.

Night had fallen softly outside, enveloping the world in a soothing darkness, while the dimmed lights of the bus created a warm, intimate ambience. Kenneth turned to Dihya, his eyes catching the soft glow of the lamps.

- I'm really happy to have met you today, Dihya, he says, his voice full of sincerity. You're a special person.

Dihya, touched by his words, offered him a tender smile.

- Me too, Kenneth. It's been an extraordinary day, thanks in part to you.

The rest of the journey unfolded in perfect harmony, a mixture of deep conversations and complicit silences. The discreet purr of the engine and the regular rocking of the bus helped to create an atmosphere of tranquility and closeness.

Halfway there, the bus slowed to a stop at a small station near Stratos Villas, Dihya's place of residence. She turned to Kenneth, a wistful smile floating on her lips.

- This is where I get off, she said softly.

Kenneth, a little surprised and sorry to see their moment come to an end, returned his smile.

- I hope we can meet again soon.

Dihya nodded, her eyes shining with sincerity.

- I hope so too, Kenneth.

Kenneth got up to help her take her bag down from the luggage compartment. Then, gently taking Dihya's hand, he whispered:

- Thank you for an incredible day.

- Thank you, Kenneth. See you soon, replied Dihya, her hand briefly squeezing his before releasing it.

She stepped off the bus, giving Kenneth one last look before the doors closed. Kenneth sat down again, looking out of the window as the bus restarted. A mixture of sadness and anticipation washed over him, sensing that this moment marked the beginning of something special between them.

When the bus finally reached the port of Chania, Kenneth disembarked, tired but happy, the unspoken promise of seeing each other again soon floating in his mind. Memories of Dihya and shared moments brightened his thoughts, and he was already looking forward to seeing her again, convinced that this budding relationship was only just beginning.

Chapter 29

Dihya had landed on the island a week before Kenneth. The itineraries concocted by the tour operator differed slightly, forcing them to wait three interminable days before their paths crossed again. In the meantime, each was scrupulously following his detox program.

On this particular day, Kenneth had a date with the ocean for a scuba diving session. Donning his neoprene wetsuit, he adjusted his mask and regulator with the expertise of a regular before slipping into the crystal-clear waters of Agios Onoufrios, a renowned dive site near Chania. The excitement of discovering the secrets of the deep was palpable. As soon as he dived in, Kenneth was enveloped by the spellbinding beauty of the rock formations and coral reefs, home to a myriad of marine creatures. The brilliant colors of the fish, the ballet of the anemones and the play of light filtering through the water captivated his senses. Yet, between each stroke of the fins, his thoughts wandered to Dihya. He saw her sparkling eyes and warm smile again, adding a bittersweet note to the wonder of his dive.

Exploring an underwater cavern with walls lined with sponges and soft corals, the bubbles from his respirator rose in a rhythmic dance towards the surface, composing a soothing aquatic symphony. Despite the hypnotic splendor of the environment, Kenneth couldn't help thinking about the next time he'd see Dihya, when he'd be able to chat with her and share unforgettable moments. During a break near a wreck, he floated peacefully, watching the schools of fish. The serenity of the water contrasted with the tumult of his emotions. He remembered their last conversations on the beach, on the bus, his bursts of laughter and the moments of complicity he sorely missed.

Finally, the dive was coming to an end. Kenneth began his ascent, respecting the necessary decompression stops. As he surfaced, sunlight streaming down his face, he smiled as he thought of Dihya, promising himself to tell her every detail of this unforgettable underwater adventure.

Dihya's day took place some ten kilometers away, in the heart of a historic fortress. For a history graduate, the setting was ideal. The tour operator, using artificial intelligence to propose tailor-made activities, had hit the nail on the head once again.

Dihya paced the corridors of the Maritime Museum of Chania, located in the ancient Firka fortress. As soon as she arrived, she was captivated by the imposing architecture of this Venetian relic overlooking the port of Chania. Inside, she was greeted by a rich collection of maritime artifacts. The first rooms traced the naval history of Crete, displaying models of ancient ships, navigational instruments and objects recovered from the seabed. In front of a detailed model of a trireme, she lingered, admiring the ingenuity of ancient shipbuilding.

During her visit, Dihya discovered sections devoted to the Byzantine and Venetian periods, illustrating the evolution of maritime techniques and naval conflicts. Ancient maps and portraits of famous navigators captivated her attention, evoking tales of adventure and discovery. She then entered the room dedicated to the Second World War, where poignant memories of the Battle of Crete were on display. Black-and-white photographs, uniforms and military equipment told the story of the soldiers' heroic battles and sacrifices. Emotion overwhelmed her as she read the testimonies of the survivors and observed the personal objects of the combatants.

At the heart of the exhibition, a display case particularly caught her eye: it contained fragments of shipwrecks and everyday objects found in the depths of the sea, each piece bearing the marks of time and history. Dihya imagined the stories these objects could tell, their journey through the ages and across the seas.

As she walked through the halls, her thoughts occasionally wandered to Kenneth. She wondered how his diving was going and hoped he was as amazed by underwater discoveries as she was here. The beauty and serenity of the museum contrasted with the excitement of diving, but both shared a common quest for discovery and connection with history and nature.

On her way out of the museum, Dihya paused to admire the panoramic view of the port from the fortress. The fading sun bathed Chania in a golden light. She breathed deeply, soaking up the atmosphere steeped in history, before heading for the exit. Kenneth's hotel room was a stone's throw away, but he was on the north side of the island. She felt a certain regret. What if she stayed and waited for him? The idea crossed her mind, but she quickly came to her senses. She could wait three days, she who had been single for years. So she returned to Stratos Villas, her hotel, with a pinch of bitterness.

During the day, the lovers were separated, each on their own itinerary, far from each other. But paradoxically, when night fell, it was a different story altogether. Calls were forbidden, so they spent hours texting. Occasionally, they discovered that video messages were not blocked. So, they recorded and sent videos to each other.

Despite attempts at censorship, the humans always found a way around...

Their burgeoning passion drove them mad, and made them forget the purpose of their stay: digital detox. While they were supposed to be away from their screens, they were spending sleepless nights glued to them.

The digital detox on the island of Crete is actually quite symbolic, going back to ancient times. Like Icarus and Daedalus in Greek mythology, participants were taken there to be deprived of a certain freedom, a punishment they had to accept without questioning, on pain of regret.

***

Daedalus and his son Icarus, trapped on the island by Minos' vengeance, desperately tried to escape. Daedalus, with his inventive genius, built wings by attaching feathers to wax, hoping to fly to freedom. Before setting off, he warned his son not to fly too close to the sun, as the wax would melt, nor too close to the sea, where the humidity would weigh down the wings. But intoxicated by the exhilaration of flying, Icarus forgot his father's advice. Climbing ever higher, he approached the sun, and the heat melted the wax. The feathers came loose, and Icarus fell to his death in the waves below.

***

On this island steeped in myth and legend, Kenneth and Dihya were living their own adventure. The parallel with Icarus was striking: in their quest for connection and love, would they forget the warnings and reasons for their presence here? Kenneth, like Icarus, risked burning his wings by getting too close to this forbidden passion, defying the rules established for their own good.

The future was uncertain. Would Kenneth and Dihya lose themselves in this frantic quest, sacrificing their goal of digital detox on the altar of their budding love? Or would they find a balance, like Daedalus, learning to navigate carefully between desire and reason? Only the island, with its secrets and age-old teachings, could reveal their destiny.

Chapter 30

It had been a quiet week for Kenneth, but for the past three days his phone had been vibrating wildly. Incessant SMS and video exchanges with a certain Dihya had suddenly invaded his phone.

Tarakna, who had been spying on Kenneth's every move since he left Paris, couldn't miss a beat. He quickly realized that Kenneth had met someone in Crete. This new love affair upset his carefully laid plans for *catfishing*.

Conquering an already captured heart was no easy task. But far from being discouraged, Tarakna saw an unhoped-for opportunity. A cold gleam lit up his eyes as he considered an alternative plan. Admittedly more complex and riskier, but the repercussions would be far more destructive for his target. His targets now, since a collateral victim, Dihya, was at stake too. If this new scheme succeeded, the damage would be profound and perhaps irreversible.

Chapter 31

Once again, the day promised to be rich in discoveries for the group in search of digital detox. A boat trip was planned, with Kenneth and Dihya among the participants.

The morning dawned sunny in Chania. In the bright sunshine, the ten participants, all excited about the adventure ahead, converged on the Venetian port. Kenneth, staying at the nearby Casa Delfino, was the first to arrive. Elpida, their warmly smiling guide, welcomed them enthusiastically and gave them a detailed safety briefing, setting out the rules to be observed on board and the day's itinerary. Once they had assimilated the instructions, the group boarded the Nautilus, a modern, comfortable yacht. Stavros, the captain, waved goodbye before casting off. Slowly, the boat pulled away from the quay, offering a splendid view of the colorful facades and mountains in the background. The calm, crystal-clear sea promised a pleasant crossing. Stavros steered the Nautilus towards their first port of call: the secluded cove of Seitan Limania. There, they dived into the crystal-clear waters, exploring the seabed with the snorkeling equipment provided. The multicolored fish and underwater rock formations fascinated all members of the group.

After a moment of bathing and relaxation, they set sail again for the Dikteon caves. Using a dinghy, they entered these spectacular caves, where the sun's rays played on the limestone walls, creating hypnotic reflections. Some, like Kenneth, ventured to swim in these mystical waters, feeling like daring explorers.

Back on the Nautilus, a feast awaited them. A sumptuous lunch of Cretan mezze, freshly grilled fish, juicy fruit and local wines was served. They enjoyed themselves, sharing their impressions and wonders of the morning, while preparing for the next discoveries of what promised to be an unforgettable day.

After lunch, some relaxed on deck, enjoying the bright sunshine and caressing sea breeze, while others plunged back into the crystal-clear waters for one last invigorating swim. With quiet determination, Stavros set course for the island of Thodorou, an unspoilt nature reserve where they could observe wild goats and admire the exceptional richness of the region's biodiversity.

The return trip to Chania turned out to be an enchanting experience. The sun began its majestic descent towards the horizon, tinting the sky with an array of golden and orange hues. The group, seated on the polished wooden deck, let themselves be captivated by this grandiose natural spectacle, sharing moments of silence and deep contemplation.

Kenneth and Dihya, hitherto reserved, gradually drew closer. They sat side by side, and soon Kenneth was tenderly embracing Dihya, holding her close with sensitive affection. They conversed with a new-found ease, evoking the splendor of the landscapes they were discovering, the adventures that awaited them on their return to Paris, and weaving together plans for the future with shared enthusiasm.

Dihya and Kenneth, as if called to order by an invisible force, began a serious discussion about their detox stay and the implacable reality of its likely long-term failure.

- Now that I know you, I have no reason to spend hours on the web, Kenneth declared with a confident smile. We'll spend our time together after work instead of surfing the Net like vagabonds.

- For you, maybe, replied Dihya, a hint of concern in her voice. But for me, I spend too much time monitoring social networks and responding to criticism from my detractors about my investigations! It's inevitable for a journalist these days. Buzz is the best way to spread information on a large scale. Without it, all news is useless. Nobody reads the press anymore. We're moderate junkies before we become real junkies. I wonder if I shouldn't change profession. Remember the precise rule our guide explained to us: without a change of environment, relapse is almost inevitable. If I continue to have a PC in front of me for eight hours a day, relapse is guaranteed!

Kenneth nodded, his expression more serious.

- What else would you like to do if you really had to change? You've already done it, and you're experienced in career changes.

- I don't know, replied Dihya with a sigh. But taking a farm at the end of the world with a few animals wouldn't do me any harm!

Kenneth burst out laughing.

- Of course not, who's going to bring down the corrupt if people like you stop being journalists?

- Well, I don't care, replied Dihya with a defiant gleam in her eye. All the people have to do is get off their butts and pass laws to prevent it. In Scandinavian countries, a minister resigns over

€400 in private expenses incurred with his civil servant's card. That's all we need here. That's it!

- Yes, but someone, a journalist like you, has to reveal this information before the Minister is forced to resign, Kenneth pointed out insistently.

Dihya was silent for a moment, thinking.

- Ah yes, you're right. We investigative journalists are indispensable in the end. And that explains why I'm still here, at the Herald, while all my former colleagues who only did editorial work have disappeared, replaced by AI.

***

Gone are the days when freelancers would copy and paste AP or Reuters dispatches. From now on, each media outlet will be equipped with artificial intelligence capable of personalizing the information provided by these press agencies, adjusting it according to its editorial line. For example, when the accession to power of a democrat figure is announced, the New York Times headlines "A shift and doubts about the country's future", while the New York Post headlines "A victory and a lot of hope". Two almost contradictory interpretations of the same news item, each aimed at satisfying the expectations of its readership.

***

- What about me? Should I stop too? questioned Kenneth, intrigued.

- You don't need the Internet as much, retorted Dihya with a mischievous smile. Otherwise, all you have to do is follow me to the farm.

The two lovers burst out laughing, relishing the idea of a bucolic adventure, alone in their bubble. Absorbed in their complicity, they didn't even notice that the Nautilus was docking. It was Stavros' sounding of the foghorn that brought them back to the reality of their group life.

Elpida warmly thanked each member of the crew and distributed souvenir photos taken during the day. The passengers left the boat with their hearts full of unforgettable memories, ready to continue their promising stay.

Standing on the lighthouse-lit quay, Kenneth and Dihya were bathed in an intermittent light, reflecting their current state of mind, torn between hope and uncertainty as to the next step that could well be decisive for the continuation of their adventure. In a gentlemanly gesture, Kenneth offered Dihya to spend the night with him, his hotel being just a few steps away, while Dihya's was some thirty kilometers away. Dihya's face lit up with happiness, despite her efforts to conceal it. She accepted in a shy but deeply expressive voice. Eyes closed, she lifted her chin slightly, inviting Kenneth to kiss her. He leaned in and kissed her tenderly, uniting their lips in a passionate embrace. The seashell trinkets of the souvenir vendors gently tinkled in the sea breeze, adding a poetic touch to the moment. Visual and aural fireworks seemed to celebrate a growing love.

Chapter 32

Tarakna contemplated his new plan with icy determination. Two words echoed in his mind like a mantra: *double deepfake*. The concept was both simple and terrifying in its execution. Tarakna planned to clone the two lovers, Dihya and Kenneth, at the same time. Kenneth, convinced that he was talking to his beloved, would in fact be talking to an AI, a digital clone of Dihya. At the same time, Dihya, believing she was talking to her beloved Kenneth, would also be duped by an AI.

To carry out this bold plan, Tarakna needed data, lots of data. He needed an astronomical amount. Like a spider spinning its web, he had embarked on a frantic collection, scanning the web from top to bottom in search of every publication, every photo, every word exchanged by his targets. After dozens of hours of intense calculations on his powerful machine, he was finally ready.

Kenneth was no problem. Tarakna had already collected an enormous mass of data from his phone: videos, images, texts of all kinds. It was an invaluable manna that would greatly facilitate the creation of the male AI. But for Dihya, the situation was different. He didn't yet have enough information to create a credible clone. The conversations captured between Kenneth and Dihya would be crucial to the success of his plan. He integrated every word, every nuance of their exchanges into his AI training, hoping to fill in the gaps.

However, Tarakna was no fool. He knew that despite all his precautions, certain details could betray his diabolical plot. Perfection was hard to achieve, even for an ace like him. Yet he had no choice. Every minute counted. He plunged into the final adjustments, aware that failure was not an option.

In the shadows of his lair, Tarakna observed the first simulations of his creations. The AIs were beginning to take shape, their conversations becoming more fluid, more human. A smile appeared on his face, a sign that boded ill for Kenneth and Dihya.

As the days passed, Tarakna's plan took shape. He constantly monitored the progress of both instances of Asklepios, correcting errors, fine-tuning details. The fateful moment was approaching. Kenneth and Dihya, unaware of the menacing shadow hovering over them, continued their frenetic SMS and video exchanges, unaware that every word they spoke brought them a little closer to the web of lies Tarakna was weaving around them.

Tension mounted with each passing day. Tarakna knew that the slightest flaw could ruin weeks of intense preparation. Yet excitement drove him forward. He wondered how the lovers would react when they discovered the truth. But perhaps they would never discover it, trapped in a digital labyrinth with no way out. Together, would they be the new Icarus of modern times who had burnt his wings?

As night fell over the city, Tarakna, in the half-light of his den, looked forward to the day when his plan would finally be put to the test.

Chapter 33

Night had long since spread its dark mantle over the old port, but Kenneth and Dihya continued to converse with a fervor that seemed to defy the hours. The mild climate of the evening seemed to invite them to open up to each other. The magic of their idyllic setting was only enhanced by their deep connection, each encounter becoming a precious opportunity to share fragments of their existence.

Invariably, however, their discussions returned to what was tormenting them both: their addiction to screens. It had become a kind of Godwin point, the inevitable subject that always came up.

Dihya, after a moment's reflection, shared a personal observation with disarming sincerity:

- For me, it's become a mechanical habit. As soon as I open my eyes in the morning, my first thought is for my phone. I check social networks compulsively, looking for the slightest novelty.

And when I feel stressed or blocked, my mind automatically turns to this poison. What's even more absurd is that I know there's nothing really interesting to be found there most of the time. It's all purely mechanical, without the slightest thought.

Kenneth nodded, an expression of understanding on his face:

- You're not alone in this, believe me. We've all become mechanical oranges.

Dihya smiled sadly before retorting:

- That's well said, but you're too lenient with the term oranges. I would have called them tomatoes. They're much more fragile. Once they've fallen, they can't withstand the shock.

The two lovers exchanged a knowing glance, aware that behind the humor lay a disturbing truth about their modern condition. Kenny smiled, because he understood that Dihya didn't know what he was talking about, for once.

- We're not thinking of the same oranges, he clarified. I grew up near Glasgow, as I told you, and this city has the third oldest subway in the world, after London and Budapest. It's called *Clockwork Orange* because of the color of the cars. It has a rare peculiarity, less than a dozen similar cases in the world: it is circular with two loops. Trains on the inner loop turn clockwise indefinitely, and those on the outer loop counter-clockwise. It's like two earthworms orbiting a central point, with mechanical guts of course.

- I love your metaphor. We go round and round like machines, without really knowing why. And then we tell ourselves we're free. What a joke! To paraphrase Spinoza, if oranges could think, they'd say they were free to fall.

- I agree with you, with one nuance, retorted Kenneth. Spinoza was talking about *rolling stones*. These stones move in directions governed only by the laws of physics. When they fall, ironically enough, we speak of "free fall". Of course, the stones have no control over their destiny. Nor does anyone intervene in any way. And that's the difference with us.

Kenny stood back slightly, his gaze lost in the meandering of his memories. The light reflected from the harbour waters played on his face, accentuating the shadow of a deep thought.

Dihya nodded, touched by melancholy. They stood there in silence, contemplating the invisible workings of their existence, united in this elusive quest for freedom.

- Perhaps we too are stones. Stones that are aware of their downfall, but which, in spite of it all, seek meaning in their perpetual movement.

Dihya agreed, but there was a glimmer of uncertainty in her eyes.

- I followed the beginning, but I don't see what you're getting at, she said, her tone revealing curiosity mixed with impatience.

Kenneth, sensing the importance of the moment, took a deep breath before continuing.

- Let's get back to the train, the *Clockwork Orange*, as it's called where I come from. The name actually has another origin. A movie, to be precise, directed by the famous Stanley Kubrick in the 1970s.

Dihya raised an eyebrow, a gleam of recognition in her eyes.

- You're talking about Stanley Kubrick, the director of "2001: A Space Odyssey", right?

Kenneth nodded with a smile.

- Yes, that's the one. He made a film called Clockwork Orange, based on a futuristic novel by British writer Anthony Burgess. I can summarize the story for you if you like. Unless you'd rather watch it, in which case I won't spoiler.

Dihya, still puzzled, but eager to get back to their original topic, replied:

- Go ahead, but don't forget to get back on topic.

Kenneth, aware of the promise implicit in his gaze, reassured her.

- Don't worry, that's precisely why I want to talk to you about it.

In love as he was, Kenneth spared no effort to please Dihya. So, he set about summarizing the story as he remembered it, every word carefully chosen, every detail thought out to capture her attention while drawing her inescapably back to the point he wanted to make.

***

Clockwork Orange focuses on a young delinquent, Alex DeLarge, fascinated by violence and the music of Beethoven, navigating a decadent and violent urban world. Alex's psychological journey unfolds in three main acts:

Act 1: Anarchic enjoyment

Alex DeLarge is a complex character whose deviant pleasures are intrinsically linked to a quest for power and domination. His passion for Beethoven, particularly the 9^e Symphony, reflects a duality between an appreciation of artistic beauty and a perverse use of this admiration to amplify his violent acts. His acts of violence are executed with a certain theatricality, as evidenced by the rape he committed while singing "Singing in the Rain". This juxtaposition of classical culture and ultraviolence underlines a psyche where aestheticism is perverted by brutality.

Act 2: Repression and manipulation

Alex's capture and treatment by the justice system marks a turning point in his psychological development. The "Ludovico technique", an aversive therapy, aims to eradicate his violent tendencies by associating images of violence and sex with intense physical pain. This Pavlovian conditioning temporarily transforms Alex into a harmless being, incapable of violence or sexual desire. However, this forced suppression of his free will and natural impulses raises profound ethical questions about choice and morality. The treatment does not rehabilitate Alex, but makes him vulnerable and manipulable. His good will and honesty are involuntary; he functions like a mechanical orange, organic on the outside and mechanical on the inside.

Act 3: Resurgence and manipulation

On his release from prison, Alex is confronted with a society that has rejected and transformed him. He is defenseless against those he once dominated. His meeting with Mr. Alexander, one of his former victims, and the latter's attempt to use him to discredit the government, reveal a new form of manipulation. The use of the 9^e Symphony to drive Alex to suicide is psychological revenge, exploiting the residual effects of the Ludovico technique.

Alex's return to hospital, followed by the Home Secretary's proposal, symbolizes a final manipulation in which Alex becomes a propaganda tool. His return to his former impulses for violence and sex, while serving the interests of an opportunistic government, illustrates a cynical victory of society over the individual.

To sum up, Alex DeLarge's story explores themes of free will, social repression and psychological manipulation.

***

Dihya smiled slightly, like someone being told a carefully guarded secret.

- I now understand what you were trying to get across to me. We're all like poor Alex, conditioned not by the laws of nature, but by the insidious power of digital platforms. All these applications, combining technological advances and psychological knowledge, are designed to maximize our time spent in front of screens.

- That's exactly it, Kenneth replied gravely. Alex's conditioning was so intense that he eventually attempted to take his own life. Stanley Kubrick described his film as a social satire, raising the question of whether behavioral psychology and psychological conditioning could become formidable weapons in the hands of a totalitarian government seeking to exert absolute control over its citizens, turning them into mere automatons. Replace government with the big digital platforms, whose aim is not totalitarian control, but pure and simple profit, and the result is the same. The more time we spend on these applications, the more revenue they generate from advertising. We are reduced to robots, playing slot machines where the currency we insert is our attention, our available brain time.

Dihya felt a wave of sadness wash over her as she listened to Kenneth's words. She had thought herself mistress of her destiny, but now found herself almost powerless. Have I become a machine with no real free will? she asked herself inwardly. She rested her head on Kenneth's shoulder and closed her eyes, seeking some semblance of comfort in the gesture.

Chapter 34

Kenneth enveloped Dihya in an embrace full of softness and desire, as if he wanted to protect her from a barely perceptible sea breeze. Through the thin fabric of Dihya's shirt, he felt her nipples harden, reminiscent of ripe, tempting cherries. Their bodies brushed against each other, the warmth of their proximity awakening a burning passion between them. His delicate caresses on Dihya's hands provoked shivers of pleasure, and her body's response only accentuated the desire rising within him. Every gesture, every touch became a promise of intense moments to come, a sensual dance where every movement brought their souls a little closer together.

- You must be hungry, Kenneth suggested with a smile. I'll buy you dinner.

- I'm starving, let's go, she replied enthusiastically.

- I've discovered a charming place. Follow me.

They headed for the PALLAS restaurant on the harbour. The evening promised to be magical and romantic. The setting was idyllic: a seaside restaurant offering a panoramic view of the boats rocking on the waves. The clear, star-studded sky added a touch of enchantment, while the sea breeze provided a welcome coolness on this balmy night. Seated at a terrace table near the water, under a pergola elegantly decorated with dimmed lights and climbing plants, Kenneth and Dihya were enveloped in a warm, intimate atmosphere, accentuated by candlelight. The soothing murmur of the waves and the laughter of passers-by formed a harmonious background.

The PALLAS menu offered a delicate fusion of Mediterranean and Cretan cuisine. Kenneth and Dihya began by savoring a variety of mezzes: marinated olives, creamy tzatziki, dolmas and grilled feta cheese. Then they enjoyed a carpaccio of fresh fish, finely seasoned with local herbs. For the main course, Dihya opted for a seafood risotto flavored with saffron, while Kenneth chose a fillet of sea bream accompanied by grilled seasonal vegetables. The dishes, beautifully presented, exploded with flavor, intoxicating the taste buds of both lovers.

Between each bite, Kenneth and Dihya exchanged knowing glances and tender smiles, discussing their dreams, plans and the memories they were building together. The waiter, discreet and attentive, made sure their evening was perfect, regularly checking that nothing was missing.

The evening concluded with light desserts: vanilla panna cotta with red fruit coulis for Dihya and a plate of baklava for Kenneth, accompanied by strong, aromatic Greek coffee. The gentle melodies of a local musician added the finishing touch to this enchanting evening.

As they left the restaurant, Kenneth and Dihya felt closer than ever, their love intensified by this culinary experience and the unique atmosphere of the port of Chania. Hand in hand, they headed for Casa Delfino, anticipating a night that promised to be short, but full of tender memories.

Chapter 35

At dawn, Kenneth was roused from his restless sleep by the shrill ringing of his telephone. Exhausted by a tumultuous night, he decided not to answer, ignoring the urgency of the situation. It was a fatal error: the Paris police were desperately trying to reach him. The password he had given them to access his computer was incorrect. Worse still, the contents of his hard disk were encrypted, making access impossible without the key. The agents could try to crack the code, but this would take considerable time, depending on the complexity of the password.

Tarakna, true to his meticulous habit, had planned everything. Knowing Kenneth's old password from the malware he'd installed to spy on his activities, he'd made only one minor change to the code: he'd deleted one letter, transforming "Magali@1996" into "Magalia1996". This clever modification offered a double advantage. On the one hand, it saved the police some time, as the shortened password would be easier to decipher. On the other hand, it suggested that Kenneth was playing on the ambiguity between the "@" symbol and the letter "a" to fool them.

When the police discovered this subterfuge, they would be convinced that Kenneth had deliberately provided an incorrect password to save time, sowing further doubt and amplifying suspicion against him. And when the investigators viewed the firm's surveillance camera recordings, stored on the computer, they would be confronted with irrefutable proof of Kenneth's involvement in the heinous crime that had taken place there. The trap was perfectly set, and Tarakna relished the thought of the confusion and growing guilt that would soon overwhelm Kenneth.

Chapter 36

After a restless night, Kenneth awoke with difficulty, his body numb with fatigue and still vivid memories of the passionate hours gone by. He glanced absent-mindedly at his phone and noticed two missed calls. Their anonymous origin aroused only a slight frown in him. After all, there was nothing he could do about it, as anonymous calls remained out of his reach, and even if they did, it was impossible for him to contact anyone because of the constraints of his detox stay.

Dihya, snuggled up against his powerful chest, was still fast asleep. The sweetness of her sighs betrayed the delicious exhaustion of a night of intoxicating love. Perhaps she was still savoring these moments in a never-ending dream. Kenneth, with infinite tenderness, caressed her with his fingertips, his gestures slowly tracing the delicate curves of her breasts. He placed a light, loving kiss on her forehead, his lips grazing her skin with softness and desire. He contemplated her soothed face for a moment, then, with infinite caution, gently detached himself, spreading his head so as not to disturb her sleep, and stood up.

He headed for the bathroom, where a hot shower soothed his tense muscles. The contact of the water against his skin invigorated him, erasing the last vestiges of sleepiness. Once ready, he made his way to the hotel restaurant. He filled a tray with golden pastries, fresh fruit, a cup of steaming coffee and another of fragrant tea before silently making his way back to his room.

Dihya, now awake but still languid on the bed, looked up at him as he entered, arms full.

- Hello darling, how are you? he asked, a tender smile lighting up his face.

- Hi Kenny, I'm fine, thanks, she replied, her eyes sparkling with recognition.

- I hope you like croissants. Your coffee's here, he says, pointing to the steaming mug on the tray.

- Thank you, that's kind, she murmured in return, her lips stretching into a gentle smile.

Kenneth approached and placed a kiss on her lips before inviting her to get up. Dihya slipped away to the bathroom, and returned a few moments later, wrapped in a fluffy bathrobe. Together, they sat down to a simple but delicious breakfast, a moment of shared calm after a tumultuous night.

The two lovers were having breakfast, reminiscing about the night's events. Between bursts of laughter and teasing, time flew by. Once the meal was over, Kenneth invited Dihya to follow him, eyes closed, promising a little surprise. He asked her to let him guide her.

Confident, Dihya followed him, her eyes tightly shut. She felt the elevator door opening and the rapid ascent of the lift. She guessed they were going up, without knowing exactly where they were going.

- Just a few more steps and we'll be there, murmured Kenneth.

Exiting the elevator, they climbed a few more steps before reaching a large, flat surface. Kenneth adjusted Dihya's position slightly and asked her to open her eyes.

Dihya marveled at the panoramic view of Chania from the hotel terrace. The harbor, with its lighthouse and boats, stretched out in splendor. On the other side, houses as far as the eye could see, with their ochre-tiled roofs, formed a maze of narrow streets reminiscent of the Casbah or ancient Mediterranean quarters. Below the terrace, the hotel's courtyard, adorned with pebble frescoes, added an artistic touch to the landscape, which resembled a watercolor painting one could never tire of. The terrace itself, dotted with palm trees and various plants, resembled an oasis suspended above the ground. Turning to her left, Dihya smiled:

- You see, over there is the Firka fortress, now a naval museum. That's where I went when you were scuba diving.

- Yes, I do know. I've been there myself. It's incredible.

Kenneth let her contemplate the landscape before pointing to a distant spot with his index finger:

- Can you see this unusual monument?

- Are you talking about the mosque over there on the edge?

- Exactly.

- Yes, I can see her. She's charming, and very singular indeed.

К

***

The Hassan-Pacha Mosque, also known as the Janissary Mosque, seemed like a UFO in this city, standing there with no apparent connection to the other buildings. It was surrounded by houses built on ancient Greek ruins and hotels with names evocative of Greek mythology: Amphitriti Hotel, Pandora Suites, and others. Its many domes were reminiscent of the spherical radomes of the Echelon interception network. Its four stone arches had a unique character. It was the very first mosque erected in Crete during the Ottoman conquests, replacing an ancient Byzantine church.

***

- I'd never have guessed it was a mosque if our guide hadn't told us a few days ago, said Kenneth. It doesn't have a minaret like most other Muslim religious buildings.

- I don't know if your guide told you about it, but she originally had one, when she was built in the 17th century. It was probably destroyed at the outbreak of the Second World War, or shortly before. The building has not been used as a place of prayer since the 1920s, when all the Turkish inhabitants had to leave the island due to the exchange of populations between Greece and Turkey. This is what the Greeks call the Great Catastrophe, the culmination of the Greco-Turkish war which led to the defeat of the Greek army by Mustafa Kemal and the expulsion of one and a half million Christians from Asia Minor, while half a million Muslims had to leave Greece to settle in Turkey.

Kenneth had just been masterfully reminded that Dihya was first and foremost a historian, and what she had just said tallied perfectly with what he had heard from the guide.

- So, you know a lot about the history of this mosque, then? asked Kenneth. It must make you happy to have a building like this right here, reminding you of your Arab origins.

Kenneth thought he'd struck a chord by mentioning a bit of history, but from the look on Dihya's face, he knew something was wrong.

Chapter 37

Dihya smiled slightly and invited Kenneth to sit down on a bench with an umbrella. The sun was becoming increasingly aggressive on this exposed terrace, and a long chat seemed inevitable.

Hearing Kenneth's words, Dihya thought back to that video, a deepfake, seen by millions on the Internet and believed by all, because it seemed consistent in every way. She thought she was living in a kind of historical deepfake, an illusion that deceives the uninformed eye and brain!

***

In recent years, deepfakes have been created by exploiting the power of AI, but humans have always done the same thing. The creation of illusion has but one aim: to distort perception and impose a certain belief. This belief then imposes itself as an obvious reality, with schools often serving as a vector of authority, validation and perpetuation of this pseudo-reality.

***

- But I've never told you about my Arab origins, replied Dihya, without animosity, always with that quiet smile.

- You told me that your father emigrated to France from Algeria, didn't you?

- Yes, it's true. I did say that, but at no point did I mention Arab origins.

- I don't understand, said Kenneth, clearly puzzled. Do we agree that Algeria is a Muslim country?

- Yes, it's true. Like all North African countries, the inhabitants are mostly Muslim. But the rest is just preconceived notions in the Western collective unconscious. Will you tell a Turk that he's an Arab, when the Ottoman Empire was the culmination of Muslim expansion? Or an Indonesian who lives in the world's largest Muslim country and is therefore Arab? Of course not. They wouldn't agree, just as you wouldn't if I told you that you were German or Italian. The only country in the world with the word "Arab" in its designation is Saudi Arabia, two if you count its satellite, the United Arab Emirates. It's no coincidence, you know. There's a reason why the countries of North Africa don't use it.

- Yes, I understand now, he says, shaking his head. We do have a tendency to mix religion and ethnic origin. But that doesn't get me very far when it comes to your origins! He plunged his gaze into hers, trying to pierce the enigma.

- You're still a mystery to me, he added, his voice full of undeniable fascination.

- I'm getting there. What do you see on my chain?

- I'm no math expert, but from what I remember of high school, the first letter is a D, the Greek delta that looks like a triangle.

The others I don't remember well. But given the number of letters on the chain, five in all, it probably corresponds to your first name: Dihya. I'm guessing you had it custom-made here in Crete.

- Another belief, a beautiful story that seems ready-made and without a shadow, replied Dihya with an enigmatic smile. No, I've owned this chain for at least ten years, long before my first visit to Greece. These letters do form my first name, but they're not Greek.

- Tell me it's not true, laughed Kenneth, skeptically.

- These letters are from the Berber alphabet, *tifina*ɣ, which actually resembles Greek. It contains thirty-three letters, more than Latin or Greek, for that matter. The Berbers, or Amazighs, are the original, indigenous people of North Africa. The word Amazigh originally means "free man". Contrary to what we sometimes hear, the name "Berber" has nothing to do with "barbarian" and derives from an Amazigh term meaning "foreigner". The exonym was later adopted by the Greeks to designate other peoples, including the Amazighs. And this is what has come down to us.

Dihya took out her phone, quickly flipped through her photo album and handed it to Kenneth.

- Look at this table, this is the Berber alphabet.

Kenneth picked up the phone, observing the image with visible fascination. The characters, though foreign, possessed an archaic beauty, like a key opening the doors to a thousand-year-old history.

Kenneth stared longingly at the phone, astonished by what he had just heard.

- If I understand correctly, North Africa is inhabited by Berbers, who are Muslims, but not Arabs?

- Yes, there are Berbers, but there are also Arabs, who have arrived here since the Muslim conquests or more recently after independence. However, many Berbers are unaware of their origins. Genetic studies confirm this. In most cases, they speak Arabic and therefore think they are Arabs. In recent years, many people have sought to better understand their genealogy and have discovered an entirely different truth. For a long time, this was a taboo subject in many families. Fortunately, things have changed and people are now proudly claiming their Berber identity. That's what I'm doing right now, telling you about my true origins.

- It's amazing, replied Kenneth.

- Not really, and it's not an isolated case. In France, for example, Breton historian Mona Ozouf talks about it. Bretons used to be ashamed of their origins. Ozouf explains that this stemmed from the image portrayed by French writers of Bretons as "unwashed bodies", "coarse spirits", unable to speak their language without a gag. There's a pejorative term still used today to sum up this contempt. Do you know it?

Kenneth shook his head. He had no idea.

- It's the word "plouc". At the end of the 19th century, many Breton peasant families, faced with poverty, migrated to Paris. These migrants, often unfamiliar with the French language, were viewed with condescension by Parisians, even though they provided cheap labor. Parisians called them "ploucs", in reference to Breton localities beginning with "plou". Today, Bretons proudly assert their identity with *Breizh pride.* The Berbers of Kabylia, my region of origin, went through a similar story when they migrated to Algiers, the capital of Algeria. There were even mocking songs sung by children in Algiers.

Dihya burst out laughing, thinking of a show by the famous comedian Fellag. He evokes this reality, which he has personally experienced, in a hilarious show mixing songs and mocking dances about Berber "mountain people".

Kenneth sensed that Dihya felt strongly about the subject. His curiosity and desire to get to know his beloved better drove him to find out more.

- I'd like to discover your culture, he said softly. I've never heard of it on TV or read about it in the press or in books. I'm sorry to hear that. Can you tell me a little more about it?

Chapter 38

Dihya beamed with enthusiasm at the prospect of sharing the treasures of her native culture with Kenneth. She committed herself with palpable eagerness, diving into every detail.

- My first name alone could inspire a novel, declared Dihya with undisguised pride. Dihya, also known as Kahina, was a 7th-century Berber warrior queen. She led the resistance against the Umayyads during the Muslim conquest of the Maghreb. Her story is so powerful that many feminist novelists and essayists have adopted the figure of Kahina for her immense symbolic charge, presenting her as one of the first feminists in history. Renowned for her strength, legend has it that she possessed magical powers. Her enemies called her al-Kāhina, an Arabic term meaning "soothsayer" or "prophetess". She inflicted so many defeats on them that they came to believe she could divine their military strategies in advance.

At the famous Battle of the Camels, she succeeded in expelling the Umayyads from Ifriqiya, forcing them to take refuge in Cyrenaica for almost five years. During this period, Kahina ruled a vast independent Berber state, stretching from the Aurès mountains in present-day Algeria to the oases of Gadames in Libya.

Five years after their first attempt, the enemy troops returned in force, this time succeeding in subduing several regions. Kahina confronted them at Tabarka, in present-day Tunisia, in a battle described by the accounts as particularly ferocious. In the end, Kahina was defeated. According to some sources, she either died in battle or committed suicide. Ibn Khaldun, the famous historian, claims that she was captured and beheaded.

Kenneth listened to Dihya with undisguised admiration, before interrupting:

- But this story is worthy of a movie!

Dihya smiled, then continued.

- You know, at the Herald, some of my colleagues call me Xena, and it's not just because of my strong character.

- I imagine they know the story of the Kahina, which is very reminiscent of Xena.

- No, not really. In fact, there's an American film about it, and it's precisely in the series "Xena: Warrior Princess", in an episode of season six, if memory serves. Kahina, played by the magnificent Alison Bruce, plays the role of a desert warrior, allied with Xena to fight her enemies. As usual, Hollywood shows its mediocrity and laziness by showing Kahina fighting Romans! But then, it's not surprising. They did have the very young and famous Carthaginian general Hannibal Barca played by the sixty-something Denzel Washington, so no surprise there! Even if this actor is excellent, when talking about a historical character, it would have been fairer to choose someone more representative. But then, in Xena, they saved the honor by adorning Alison Bruce's forehead with a typically Berber piece of jewelry! Of course, there needs to be a movie specifically dedicated to Kahina and her exploits. But we're still waiting...

Kenneth interrupted Dihya with a questioning look.

- Were there other female warriors like Kahina, or is she an isolated case in Berber history?

Dihya nodded.

- There were many, but if any should be recognized as Kahina's worthy heir, it would be Fatma N'Soumer. She was another great figure of resistance, this time against the French conquest of Algeria. Ironically, she was born in the same year as the arrival of colonial troops, in 1830. At just 19 years of age, she was appointed by the Soumeur assembly, the Tajmaât, the village's political authority, to lead the Imseblen, death volunteers from numerous villages in the Djurdjura region. There was talk of 3,000 men. In 1854, they won their first battle against French forces at Tazrout, known as the Battle of Haut Sebaou, which lasted two months. The French troops, led by Generals Mac Mahon and Maissiat, numbering some 13,000 men, were defeated and forced to withdraw, leaving the surrounding villages independent. Fatma N'Soumer's reputation spread throughout Algeria. Her name was henceforth preceded by the honorific title "Lalla", out of respect. Popular poems were sung in her honor. She didn't go unnoticed with her many henna tattoos all over her body. The French called her "la Jeanne d'Arc du Djurdjura" and, guess what else? The "prophetess", like Kahina before her. Legend has it that Lalla Fatma N'Soumer had many dreams interpreted as messages from God, reminding her and the Kabyle people of their duty in the face of the invaders.

It was only in 1857, after fierce resistance at the famous battle of Icheriden, that French troops under Marshal Randon succeeded in occupying the Aït Iraten region, a first in the history of this bastion which had always resisted invaders and never lost its independence, even in the face of the Ottomans, who had been present in Algeria for three centuries. The French immediately consolidated their position after their victory by building a huge barracks and a large fort, a rampart around the town of Aït Iraten, thus giving birth to Fort-National (or Fort-Napoléon), a highly strategic area. The fort remains intact today, as does the barracks. Lalla Fatma, who continued to form a nucleus of resistance, was finally arrested in July 1857, imprisoned and placed under house arrest. She died in prison in 1863, aged 33.

- You've got to tell me more about this Berber culture, it's really fascinating, says Kenneth, his eyes shining with genuine interest.

Dihya smiled gently. Talking about any culture is usually a subject that fascinates people, but Kenneth's love for Dihya created in him a particular thirst, a deep desire to get to know her better.

- We'll talk about it later, she replies with an enigmatic smile. I'll explain everything to you tonight, but right now I've got to go to the awareness session on screen use. It's the home stretch and my departure to Paris is imminent. I'll call you back in two days.

Kenneth grimaced.

- Please don't remind me of that. I don't know how I'll get through the rest of my stay without you.

- Don't worry, she reassured him. You'll join me just a few days later and we'll have plenty of time to ourselves.

Together they went back down to the bedroom. Dihya dressed quickly before heading off to her awareness session. Kenneth, for his part, prepared for the next stage of his program, a day's volunteer work with Boroume Chania, an organization that fights food waste by redistributing surplus food to the needy.

Chapter 39

The group gathered in a spacious room, with large open windows overlooking the olive groves and surrounding hills, far from the noise of the city. There were around ten participants, each with their own unique story, but with a common goal: to disconnect from screens and reconnect with real life.

Alexios, a coach specializing in digital detox, welcomed them warmly. To lighten the mood, he starts with a little joke:

- I brought along a little box to put your phones in before the session started, but I finally remembered that you've been punished and had your Internet connection cut off. So, no need!

He then invited each member to briefly introduce themselves and share why they had decided to take part in the trip. Dihya was the third to introduce herself, talking about her work as a journalist and her need to regain balance in her life.

Alexios began the session by explaining the harmful effects of screens and social networks. He spoke of the impact on mental health:

- Anxiety and depression: constant comparisons and the pressure of social networks can lead to feelings of inadequacy and anxiety.

- Sleep disorders: blue light from screens disrupts the sleep cycle, causing insomnia.

Then he turned to physical health problems:

- Cervical pain and backache: resulting from prolonged poor posture in front of screens.

- Eye fatigue: caused by hours spent in front of screens, leading to dry, irritated eyes.

Finally, he described the impact on social relations:

- Isolation: Virtual interactions can replace face-to-face interactions, leading to a feeling of isolation.

- Reduced concentration and productivity: The constant distraction of notifications can reduce concentration.

To illustrate his point, Alexios invited several members of the group to share their stories.

Sophie, a young graphic designer, was the first to talk about how social networking had become an integral part of her work, as well as her personal life.

"At first, it was great," she says, her eyes shining with emotion. "I could share my work, receive instant feedback, and connect with other artists. But very quickly, it took a different turn. I started constantly comparing myself to others. Their success, their perfect lives... It made me anxious and depressed. I slept badly, always felt tired and couldn't concentrate on my own projects."

It was 40-year-old entrepreneur Marc's turn to add his own testimony. He explained how excessive phone use affected his relationship with his family.

"I thought I was being productive, using every minute wisely," he says. "But in reality, I was distracted all the time. I was checking email during meals, answering messages while playing with my kids. One day, my daughter said to me, 'Dad, you're here without being here.' It broke my heart. I realized I was missing out on precious moments with them."

Testimonies follow one another, and often the same observation is made about the depression resulting from social comparison between people on social networks.

Leila, a law teacher, shared her experience last, again in a similar vein. She spoke of the impact of social networks on her self-esteem.

"I'd see all these photos of people who seemed to have perfect lives. It made me feel inadequate," she says. "I'd spend hours scrolling, comparing, feeling worse and worse. I started avoiding face-to-face interactions, feeling isolated. I knew something had to change, but I didn't know how."

To further engage the group, Alexios organized interactive activities. Dihya took part in a quiz on the use of screens and social networks, then joined a group discussion where everyone shared their personal experiences. It was then that she realized how valuable collective support was.

Alexios then demonstrated relaxation techniques such as meditation and deep breathing. He guided the group through disconnection exercises, showing them how to manage screen time and limit notifications.

To help the group maintain a healthy balance, Alexios proposed concrete strategies. Used to taking quick notes, Dihya didn't miss a beat of the coach's advice. She wrote everything down in minute detail on her notepad:

1. Time Planning:

- Use time management applications to track screen use.

- Set specific times to consult social networks.

2. Healthy environment:

- Create screen-free zones, like the bedroom.

- Practice screen-free activities, such as reading, walking or creative hobbies.

3. Real connections:

- Encourage face-to-face meetings with friends and family.

- Participate in technology-free group activities, such as sports clubs or art workshops.

By the end of the session, Dihya felt inspired and ready to change her habits. Alexios concluded with a reminder of the importance of balancing screen use with other aspects of life. He once again stressed the need to rediscover the pleasure of human interaction and life without the omnipresence of screens.

She knew it wouldn't be easy, but Dihya left the room with a fresh perspective, determined to put the advice into practice.

Chapter 40

Kenneth returned very tired from his day, deeply shaken mentally. He hadn't expected to see such misery, nor to hear such poignant testimonies, when he immersed himself in the association helping the needy. The lives of executives in prestigious positions had been turned upside down overnight in the wake of the Greek debt crisis. People already in precarious situations saw their condition worsen. Many had seen their pensions or salaries drastically reduced, while others had lost their jobs, plunging them into years of misery. They turned to aid associations for food. A third of the population had fallen below the poverty line.

After a hot shower, Kenneth threw himself onto his bed. With his body sprawled out and his eyes staring at the ceiling, he began to meditate on the lives of the people here in Greece and his own in France. He relativized and considered himself a lucky man who lacked nothing and should feel happy. Especially after meeting this woman, Dihya, who would undoubtedly bring a happy upheaval to his life. Just then, Kenneth heard a knock on the door.

It was she who had just arrived. He opened the door for her and immediately hugged her before giving her a long kiss.

After a trip to the bathroom, Dihya returned wrapped in her bathrobe and sat down next to Kenneth.

- So, how was your day? asked Dihya.

- Interesting, but a bit harsh. I saw incredible misery. I didn't realize that there were people suffering so much, even though their paths seemed mapped out for a life of ease. After all, this is Europe!

- I can imagine, the effects of the 2008 crisis are still visible. But make no mistake, if you were to visit a similar organization in Paris, the Restos du Cœur for example, you'd see the same thing. It's just terrible.

- You're right, we're seeing a bit of it on the streets already. The homeless are everywhere in Paris now. It's really sad.

ⵥ

Kenneth didn't want to stir up his trying day any further. He changed the subject.

- How was your awareness session?

- Interesting too, but a real slap in the face. I didn't expect to hear some of the testimonials either, people really in pain. You'll see anyway and we'll talk about it.

Like Dihya, Kenneth would indeed follow the same session that was part of every digital detox program. He was willing to make up his own mind about it, and so preferred not to dwell on it. He finally returned to a more cheerful subject, Dihya's promise to teach him more about Berber culture.

- I'm a bit hungry, and this morning you promised to tell me more about your culture. Do you mind?

- No, don't worry. I'd love to. We'll start with a little game. Watch my chain again.

- Your chain again? She's obviously closing a lot of stories.

- Just the first letter, for your convenience. What do you see?

- We said it was the Amazigh letter Delta, like the D in Dihya.

- If you remember the word "Amazigh", that's good enough. It's the letter Delta, but it's not quite the same symbol as the one I showed you on the table. (Dihya pulls out her phone to show him the photo of the alphabet). Look closely and tell me the difference.

Kenneth smiled. He thought he knew what it was all about.

- I'm thinking of the little circle and the two little horizontal lines above the Delta. You can see them on your chain, but not in the table.

- Exactly. These little details were added at my request by the jeweller who made the chain for me. With this, it became a two-in-one chain.

Kenneth burst out laughing.

- Two chains in one, now that's something. I don't quite get it. Come on, don't keep me in suspense and tell me all about it.

- I can feel you're dying of impatience. I won't prolong your suffering. This sign symbolizes the fertility goddess Tanit, also known as *Tannou* or *Tangou*. She's equivalent of Demeter, the Greek deity. The cult of this goddess became widespread in North Africa during the Punic civilization. Traces of her can be found everywhere on monuments and ruins in Tunisia, notably in Carthage, the Punic capital. This goddess was called *Yemma* by the Berbers, meaning "mother". Later, she was sometimes called *Oumek*, an Arabic term with the same meaning. Many historians have suggested that this is the origin of the very name Tunisia. And surprise, the grand prize at the Carthage Film Festival is called The Golden Tanit!

- Interesting, but I can't see the two-in-one chain yet! interrupted Kenneth.

К

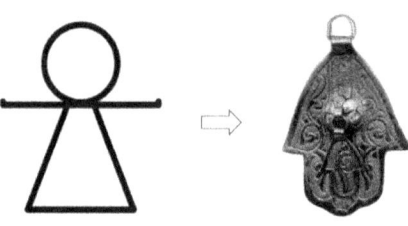

- It's a good thing you reminded me, otherwise I'd probably have lost my way. Yes, in fact the symbol of Tanit evolved over time into what would later be called *Afust*, Berber for hand. As the sign spread throughout North Africa and the Middle East, some people came to refer to it as *khamsa*, meaning five in Arabic or Hebrew, in reference, of course, to the five fingers of the hand. It's also referred to as Fatima's hand or Myriam's hand, even though Islam and Christianity had nothing to do with it in the first place. This kind of thing is even forbidden in the Muslim religion, as are all superstitions, since they are seen as interference (*shirk*) in God's powers.

The sign of Tanit is still sold today in all markets around the Mediterranean as an amulet, talisman or piece of jewelry. This symbol is supposed to protect the wearer from the evil eye.

- Do you understand now what I meant?

- Ah yes, I see. (Kenneth smiles). You're so beautiful you want to ward off the evil eye. So, you're superstitious!

- Not at all. It's above all a symbol of fertility and my origins, which suits me fine. Let me show you something else.

Dihya parted her long hair to reveal her earring.

- Look at this, it's a Berber jewel. Doesn't it remind you of something?

- Of course it is, the sign of Tanit or Fatima's five-fingered hand.

- Exactly. This motif is omnipresent in Berber jewelry. Girls wear them to make themselves look beautiful, and even more so by displaying several, of various types, all over their bodies at their weddings, an event naturally linked to fertility. And I've chosen to wear them today.

The two lovers burst out laughing before Kenneth caught the ball on the rebound.

- Is this a marriage proposal or something?

- Of course!

- Are you serious?

- Of course not, I'm just kidding. I wear them from time to time to please myself. As proof, I brought them back in my luggage when I didn't know I was going to meet you.

Kenneth understood that Dihya was making a point. He almost felt a little regret, even though he knew very well that it would be unreasonable to think of marriage right now.

Chapter 41

Kenneth felt as if he'd been transported on a journey through time, immersed in a foreign culture he'd known nothing about just a few days ago. He wanted more.

- You mentioned the cult of Tanit. I don't suppose anyone in North Africa celebrates or believes in that legend any more. Unless you make a profit out of it, like we Scots do with our Nessie, the Loch Ness monster. It attracts tourists from all over the world and makes money!

Kenneth winked at Dihya, who laughed.

- Yes, it is. It's a tradition still celebrated during periods of drought in certain regions of North Africa, notably Tunisia, under the name *Oumek Tangou*. It involves the use of a doll-shaped statuette that children take from house to house, singing: "Oumek Tango, oh women, ask God to make it rain". As you can see, it has been distorted from its original form to conform a little to Muslim belief by invoking God and not Tanit.

This tradition seems to be a variation of an even older celebration dedicated to the most powerful god of Berber mythology, the rain god *Anzar*. The tradition has come down to us through the rite of "*Tislit n Anzar*" (Anzar's fiancée). It is still celebrated today during periods of drought. Little girls make dolls and dress them up in beautiful clothes to represent the moon goddess, who offered herself to the god Anzar and spread fertility on Earth. The girls then walk around the village singing. Today, any Berber would tell you that *tislit* is the term used to designate a bride, and *tayri*, a term derived from the name of the moon goddess (*Ayyur*), is synonymous with the word *love*.

Deepfake

- Anzar is reminiscent of Poseidon, the god of the sea in Greek mythology, says Kenneth.

- Indeed, it's so reminiscent of Poseidon that one can legitimately wonder if there isn't a deep connection between the two, replies Dihya with an enigmatic smile. And the reality goes beyond mere suspicion. There are undeniable connections between ancient Berber beliefs and Greek, Roman and, of course, Egyptian mythologies.

Referring to the West's undisputed source on the ancient history of the Mediterranean basin, Dihya quoted Herodotus.

- The "father of history" himself reports that the Libyans, as he called the Berbers of antiquity, had taught the Greeks the art of harnessing four horses to a wagon. The Greeks of Cyrenaica, in what is now Libya, built temples dedicated to the Libyan god Ammon rather than to their own god Zeus. Later, they came to equate Zeus with Ammon, and some continued to worship this god under the name of Ammon-Zeus, a fusion of the two deities' traits. The cult of this god was so widespread among the Greeks that even Alexander the Great proclaimed himself "son of Zeus" in the temple of Siwa, dedicated to Ammon.

Dihya paused to let the weight of these words sink in.

- The Siwa oasis, she points out, is located in Egypt, close to the Libyan border, and is still inhabited by Berbers today. It's fascinating to see how these ancient beliefs and cultures intertwine throughout history, isn't it?

Ancient historians report that several Greek deities had Libyan origins. Athena, one of the principal goddesses of the Greek pantheon, is a notable example. Known as the goddess of war and technique, Athena was considered by many ancient historians, including Herodotus, to have Libyan roots. These accounts suggest that she was originally worshipped by the Libyans around Lake Tritonis, the largest salt plain in the Maghreb, where, according to Libyan legend, she was born of the god Poseidon. The Greeks attached such importance to Athena that they went so far as to claim that Zeus, king of the gods, had fathered her himself.

Herodotus also mentions that the aegis and Athena's clothing were typically those of Berber women. This legendary weapon, the Aegis, was nothing other than the goatskin dress worn by the Libyan women of the author's time. According to several commentators, the Aegis was made from the skin of the goat Amalthea, Zeus' nurse. When Amalthea died, Zeus took her skin and put it on his aegis.

- And guess what we call goats in Berber? asked Dihya. Well, simply *eγid* (the γ being the equivalent of the letter g, gamma). From now on, whenever you hear the expression "under the aegis of the United Nations" on the news, you'll think of the Berber origin of the word aegis!

Kenneth, his eyes wide with surprise, replied:

- It's really amazing. You wouldn't happen to have another word like that, widely used, but whose Berber origin is unknown to the general public?

- Of course, I can offer you plenty, but I don't want to look like a chauvinist either, she replied with a wry smile.

- Come on, just one and we'll move on, insisted Kenneth with a smile.

- If you're so inclined, I'll quote you another. The Old Continent owes its name to Europa, a Phoenician goddess living in the Near East. Zeus, king of the gods, kidnapped her and brought her here to Crete, giving the continent of Europe its name. The story of Africa is similar, taking its name from the Berber goddess *Ifri*.

In the aftermath of the Second Punic War, following the victory of the Romans and Numidians over the Carthaginians, the goddess Ifri was adopted by the Roman pantheon under the Latinized name "Africa". This term seems to be related to the Berber word "taferka", meaning land or property, and its owner, Aferkaw, would have given "africanus" in Latin. In Arabic, this name became "*Ifriqiya*", designating Africa in its modern sense.

A symbol of fertility, Ifri is depicted on frescoes in the many ruins of North Africa. She often holds a cornucopia and an ear of wheat, similar to Demeter, the Greek goddess of the harvest. Even today, several villages bear the Ifri name.

One of the most powerful Amazigh tribes of the Middle Ages, the *Ath Ifrene* (plural of Ifri), served a queen. Guess who she was. You know her, I'm sure.

- What are you talking about? I have no idea! replied Kenneth.

- Well, it was Queen Dihya. Everything I say is easily verifiable. One day, I'll invite you to Tunisia. We'll visit the *El Djem* museum, where a large mosaic depicting Ifri is on display.

- I'd love to, replied Kenneth. Whenever you like.

- You might think I know all this from my history studies, and that's largely true. But, in reality, I was lulled to sleep by my grandmother's tales. Every evening, she would tell me Berber myths. That's how these stories are passed down from generation to generation.

- You were really lucky, says Kenneth, slightly envious. I only learned about mythology at school, like all my classmates.

- It's never too late. I'll tell you bedtime stories if you like. You're my baby now!

- And it'll keep us away from our phone screens too! retorted Kenneth mischievously.

They burst out laughing, then Dihya got up to prepare two cups of tea. It was going to be a long evening...

Chapter 42

Kenneth suddenly discovered a passion for history, having never opened a textbook on the subject outside school. Love changes souls.

- Now you're talking mythology, which is fascinating. But are there any monuments or ancient ruins of Berber civilization? asked Kenneth, questioningly.

- Ruins are everywhere, from the Siwa oasis in Egypt to the Canary Islands in the west. What remains in relatively good condition are mainly funerary monuments and tombs, as people have always feared the desecration of tombs. There are also smaller objects such as statues and coins, which are easily buried and therefore protected from looting and destruction.

Dihya pulled out her phone to show Kenneth a photo.

Deepfake

- Look, it's the *Medracen*, a king's mausoleum in the Aurès region of eastern Algeria. According to local legend, Dihya often came here to meditate in front of the tomb. Medracen is the most beautiful and important Berber site in Algeria. The monument depicts Madrès (Madghis), said to be the founding father of Numidia, a large Berber kingdom, and therefore a probable ancestor of Numidian king Massinissa.

Dihya rummaged through the photo album on her phone before showing it to Kenneth.

- This is the tomb of the great Berber king Massinissa.

- Ah yes, it sounds immense. He must have been a great king indeed.

- Oh yes, much more than you'd think. Let me show you something.

Dihya walked over to her suitcase and opened it to take out a book.

Kenneth was pensive. What was this amazing story she was going to tell him again? he wondered deep down.

Dihya rummaged around in the book, looking for something, obviously a particular page. She stopped, then turned to Kenneth.

- Look, I'm going to read you a few passages from this book I bought at Athens airport. It's about Delos, a historically important Greek island. You'll be surprised yet again.

The Greeks pay tribute to the great Amazigh king Massinissa, who saved them from famine on more than one occasion by offering them free wheat. Under Massinissa's reign, Numidia opened up to international trade and military alliances. At the same time as Massinissa was giving wheat to the Greeks, he signed an agreement with Rome during the Punic War against Hannibal. He emerged victorious.

"The abundance of wheat deliveries to Rome, in particular to supply its armies, and to the Greek islands, bears witness to a surplus production encouraged by a proactive policy", explains archaeologist Farid Kherbouche.

Epigraphy tells us that Massinissa made several gifts of wheat to the inhabitants of the sacred island of Delos, which was also a hub for the grain trade.

Several inscriptions and statues dedicated to or erected in his honor attest to this; one of them was found by the archaeologist during a mission to the island. Engraved on the base of a blue marble statue, it bears witness to a dedication to Massinissa by a Rhodian named Charmylos.

This statue is located just a few steps from the Temple of Apollo, the island's most important monument, which contains other tokens of gratitude to Massinissa, such as that of Nicomedes, King of Bythinia.

Dihya then showed the clearly visible inscriptions on a photo occupying a good half-page of the book before closing it.

- I'm sure you're dying to visit this island, says Kenneth with a certain passion.

- Of course, you can imagine! replied Dihya.

Kenneth promised Dihya that he would invite her for a stay on the island of Delos on their next trip. A trip now from Crete would take too long and would not be feasible during this stay. It would require a trip to the mainland to take a ferry to Piraeus, and even a connection via the island of Mykonos to finally arrive in Delos.

- We can avoid coming back to Greece and do it closer to home, if that's important to you. I'd like that just as much, replied Dihya mysteriously...

Chapter 43

What do you mean, closer to home? You mean Berber tracks in Scotland? asked Kenneth in astonishment.

- We could just go to the British Museum. Yes, we'll find traces of my ancestors there.

- What is it? The British Museum in London?

- Yes, there's a Berber statue on display in the British Museum. It's a head that was found during the excavation of the Temple of Apollo in Cyrene (present-day Libya) in 1861, along with the remains of bronze horses. Its North African features indicate that it is a portrait of a native ruler, a person honored in Cyrene. Historians suggest that it is a portrait of Mastanabal, son of Massinissa, and that it dates from the time when Massinissa was a close associate of the King of Cyrene, the future Ptolemy VIII of Egypt. Mastanabal was a renowned athlete and it is highly likely that the work commemorates one of his victories.

Deepfake

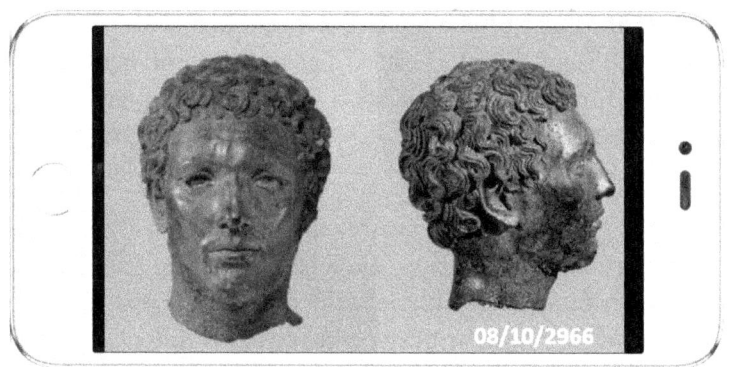

In ancient times, Numidia was considered a people of Hellenic habits and customs, and its people took part in the Panathenian Games. These games, similar to the Olympics, were reserved for Greek and Hellenized peoples. They were held in Athens. Mastanabal was crowned champion of one of these games, in the chariot racing discipline. He won 4 gold medals! He's the Léon Marchand of antiquity, or rather Zinedine Zidane, whose parents are both Berbers. Mastanabal was awarded his medal by the Greek king Nicomedes himself. A stele erected by this king, found on the island of Delos, mentions this feat and lists the winners of these games, including Mastanabal.

And the links between Berbers and the UK don't stop there. There's even more to it than that.

- What now? asked Kenneth.

- There's a British territory named after a Berber and I'm pretty sure you don't know it.

- You're probably right, but I have no idea. I really don't.

- We agree that Gibraltar is your territory. It's attached to the British crown, even if Spain continues to claim it, isn't it?

- Yes, it is. But I don't know where the name comes from.

- As part of the Muslim conquest of Spain, the leader Tariq ibn Ziyad established a bridgehead to Europe there, giving the rock its name. Gibraltar is a deformation of *Jabal-Târiq*, (*mountain of Târiq* in Arabic). Most historians agree that he was Berber, and even had a tribal origin close to that of - guess who - Queen Dihya!

According to some accounts, once he had landed in Gibraltar, Tariq had his ships burned and said to his men: "O people, where is the way out? The sea is behind you, and the enemy before you, and you have by God only sincerity and patience."

The contingent led by Tariq was mainly made up of several converted Berber tribes. Various sources mention a contingent essentially made up of local Berbers, accompanied by a few dozen Arabs charged with teaching the Koran to the newly converted soldiers.

- But it's incredible all these stories and exciting at the same time, says Kenneth again.

Since the start of their conversation, a strange detail on Dihya's phone had been troubling him deeply. At first, he'd thought it a simple coincidence, a mistake or a bug as they often say, but deep down he sensed there was something else going on, especially after all he'd heard. Every time Dihya opened a photo to show it to him, the numbers that appeared, normally supposed to indicate the date taken, seemed to correspond to something else. Although these numbers followed the format of a date, the values they displayed made no sense. He wanted to know more...

Chapter 44

To achieve the perfect deepfake, Tarakna knew he had to push his mastery of the art of *swapping* even further, i.e. transferring the current appearance of his target, Kenneth or Dihya, onto the digital clone while retaining the same clothes and voice. This technological challenge had to be accomplished in real time, as Tarakna planned to integrate the clone into live Skype communications. This task would prove far more complex than the crime he had orchestrated in Kenneth's office, where he had had access to a video recording and enough time to manipulate the video and put it back on the server without arousing suspicion.

To carry out his plan with this new constraint, Tarakna needed a super-powerful computer, capable of performing an astronomical mass of calculations per second. He ordered a machine equipped with two graphics cards, each costing $100,000. He had anticipated the long delivery times for this highly coveted type of equipment and placed his order well in advance. The beast of technology would arrive shortly.

Another major obstacle was latency, the time it took for the signal to be exchanged between his targets' devices and his server. Latency had to be kept to a minimum to avoid distortions in the video stream. Tarakna, refusing to leave anything to chance, took a radical decision: he would move to the Old Continent [Europe] to be closer to his victims, Kenneth and Dihya.

The closer the target, the better the chance of hitting it, he told himself over and over in his head...

Chapter 45

Kenneth finally decided to ask the question that had been nagging at him for some time, a strange anomaly he'd noticed on Dihya's device and had initially dismissed as a simple malfunction.

- The numbers on all the photos you showed me are incorrect, he said, pointing to the screen. They look like dates, but they're wrong. Did your phone have a bug when you took them?

- Ah yes, replied Dihya, shrugging her shoulders. I didn't even notice. It was so obvious to me that I forgot to tell you. No, there was no problem with my phone. These are the dates the photos were taken. Some of them are quite recent.

- Are you serious? exclaimed Kenneth, his eyes wide with surprise. He was beginning to wonder whether he was dealing with a mythomaniac or a delusional woman. You're talking about recent dates when we're looking at 2970?

Dihya burst out laughing, then took on a mocking air.

- Do you really believe that the Gregorian calendar is the center of the universe?

Kenneth suddenly realized that Dihya was probably right about this. After all, the Gregorian calendar had only been devised at the end of the 16th century to correct the drift of the ancient Julian calendar introduced by Julius Caesar.

- You may be right, but you owe me a slightly more detailed explanation, replied Kenneth, looking intrigued.

- Well, it's quite simple, replied Dihya, smiling. The Berbers have their own calendar, as do many other ancient civilizations. For example, the Chinese should be at something like 4700 right now, while Middle Eastern countries and Muslims in general have a counter around the year 1450. Each calendar uses an important event in history to define the year zero. For the Muslim calendar, for example, the beginning refers to the Hegira (*hijra*), i.e. the emigration of the Prophet Mohammed and his companions to the city of Medina in 622, a historic year that ushered in the era of expansion of the Muslim community.

Kenneth nodded slowly, assimilating this new perspective. He realized that his view of the world had been far too focused on his own cultural references. The idea of another, equally ancient and respected, system of time measurement seemed obvious to him now.

- So, what's the beginning for the Berbers? asked Kenneth, still looking curious.

- Once again, you may be a little surprised, replies Dihya with an enigmatic smile. The zero point of the Amazigh calendar is based on an indisputable historical fact: the enthronement as Pharaoh of Egypt of the Berber king Sheshonq I, around 950 B.C. He founded the 22nd dynasty, which ruled Egypt for more than two centuries.

- A Berber Pharaoh? Did I hear correctly?

- That's right, confirmed Dihya, shaking her head. Sheshonq I came from the Berber tribe of Mâchaouach, who lived in eastern Libya. He was not the first king of his family, but is best known for his achievements. He succeeded in unifying Egypt, and his many exploits are engraved on the famous site of Karnak. Also, a large granite sphinx bearing his name is on display at the Louvre Museum.

- Well, that's a fact established by archaeologists, says Kenneth, visibly impressed.

- Yes, there's no doubt about that, replies Dihya. Inscriptions engraved on the wall of the Karnak temple detail the conquests of Sheshonq I, including a campaign in Canaan, the territory around present-day Palestine and Israel. According to historians, Sesaq and Shishaq, two names mentioned several times in the Bible, refer to the same person, Pharaoh Sheshonq I. In the Old Testament, it is mentioned that a pharaoh named Shishaq invaded the kingdom of Judah during the reign of Rehoboam, son of Solomon. He is said to have plundered the temple in Jerusalem and carried off its treasures. But on this point, I remain suspicious. When religion gets involved, it's never serious to draw certainties!

Kenneth had already understood that Dihya, as a seasoned investigative journalist, cherished facts above all else, and she had just reminded him of this once again.

Kenneth pondered for a moment, absorbing the new information. Every detail Dihya revealed to him opened up a new perspective on history and the interweaving of different ancient civilizations.

- I imagine you're celebrating the Berber New Year in your own way, tried Kenneth.

- Of course, she replies with a touch of enthusiasm. It's called *Yennayer*, a word made up of two parts: *yan*, meaning "one", and *ayyur*, the name of the Moon goddess - remember - meaning "month". Originally, it was the day of the year in the agrarian calendar used since antiquity by Berbers throughout North Africa. In the 1980s, Berber identity activists linked this celebration to the historical event I mentioned earlier. It is celebrated between January 12 and 14, depending on the region, with numerous festivities and hearty meals, including the sacrifice of a fowl.

Dihya paused, her gaze intense, as if measuring the effect of her words.

- In Berber culture, *Yennayer* is linked to a myth known as "the old woman". Each region has its own version of this legend. The Kabyles, for example, tell of an old woman who, believing winter to be over, went out into the fields one sunny day and mocked *Yennayer*. Yennayer, furious, borrowed two days from *furar* (February) and unleashed a great storm to take his revenge.

The old woman was swept away by the waves or transformed into a stone statue, depending on the version.

Kenneth listened, fascinated by the wealth of traditions and stories that Dihya passionately unveiled. Her voice, at once gentle and determined, brought these ancient stories to life, resonating within him an insatiable curiosity for this age-old culture.

- What I'm telling you here is what people have experienced and continue to experience for centuries. In politics, on the other hand, things move more slowly. In Algeria, *Yennayer* became a paid holiday only in 2017, and was officially celebrated for the first time in 2018. In Morocco, it took even longer, until 2023. Even the Berber language, Tamazight, was long unrecognized. It only became an official language in Morocco in 2011, and has been taught in schools since 2019. In Algeria, it only became official in 2016.

Kenneth sensed emotion and a hint of regret in Dihya's voice as she spoke of this belated recognition of such a rich and ancient culture. Seeking to understand the reasons for this delay, he asked:

- What do you think are the reasons for this non-recognition?

Dihya took a breath, pausing before answering.

- The reasons are obvious enough. The region has long been under attack from neighboring countries, and each new arrival has tried to impose its own culture. It's a method of domination that goes back to the dawn of time. The best way to weaken a man or a people in order to seize their wealth is to erase their culture and memory. Fortunately, nature, sometimes more than man, knows how to protect its diversity from extinction. The mountains, the desert and its oases, just like the islands, have enabled the Berbers to survive through millennia of hostility.

The same is true of many other peoples. The desert sands have buried ancient Egyptian monuments destined for certain destruction. Today, they are revealed to us as marvels. The explosion of Mount Vesuvius was the worst thing that could have happened to the inhabitants of Pompeii in their lifetime, but in historical and cultural terms, the ashes that buried the city and its inhabitants allowed them to live on for eternity. Mother Nature knows how to protect her own in spite of everything.

Dihya's voice had softened as she spoke of this resilience, and Kenneth sensed that behind her words lay a deep pride in her people's heritage, a pride he now shared, if only a little, thanks to her.

Kenneth interrupted Dihya to agree with her.

- It's obvious. History has seen many civilizations disappear, without necessarily as a result of direct recourse to violence. Today, this soft war of influence is referred to as *soft power*. I read recently that China, whose ambition is clearly to dominate the world economically, has set up over 500 Confucius Institutes to promote the Chinese language. They are simply following the example set by others before them decades ago. The Americans are masters in this field, notably through the cinema, but not only. Programs such as *Young Leaders* enable promising young politicians from all over the world, mainly from Europe and since the 2010s from Africa and Asia, to come to the U.S. for an all-expenses-paid course of study: schooling, accommodation, meals, travel, medical care, etc. This allows them to immerse themselves in American culture and then promote it when they return home. It's very effective, judging by the systematic alignment of young European politicians with US positions, even when these are unfavorable to their own country. The return of the favor is almost mechanical!

Dihya nodded, clearly appreciating Kenneth's analysis.

- Yes, that's exactly it, Kenny. Cultural domination can be as powerful, if not more so, than domination by force. It insinuates itself into people's minds, shapes tastes and influences values. For the Berbers, it was a relentless struggle to preserve their identity in the face of these outside influences, and that struggle continues today. But thanks to their resilience and attachment to their traditions, they have been able to preserve part of their heritage. Official recognition of their culture and language is an important victory, but the battle to preserve their identity is far from over. By the way, you made me think of something when you mentioned *soft power*.

- Tell me everything, said Kenneth.

- You're absolutely right. Soft power is quite old, but the French colonial administration innovated in this area by applying a policy that could be described as anachronistic. The *French Touch*, no doubt! They arabized the names of Berber families and even regions in Algeria. Revenge, perhaps, against the people who had resisted them so fiercely? And today, ironically and in an incredible twist of history, some politicians in France - at least a good number of them - are pointing the finger at all things Arab. At the same time, Paris City Hall organizes an annual celebration of the Berber New Year. Better still, *Yennayer* has been included in France's national inventory of intangible cultural heritage since 2020!

Kenneth nodded, absorbed by this new layer of historical irony.

- It's fascinating. It shows how history is full of paradoxes. The same forces that sought to erase a culture can, decades later, recognize its value and celebrate it. It's a kind of poetic justice, albeit belated.

Dihya nodded, her gaze lost in thought.

- Yes, it's a kind of belated but precious recognition. It reminds us that this culture is resilient. Berbers have survived centuries of domination and attempts at erasure, and today we're seeing signs of recognition and respect for our heritage. This gives us hope for the future, and shows that the struggle to preserve our identity has not been in vain.

Kenneth felt a growing admiration for Dihya and her people, for their ability to resist, adapt and ultimately triumph despite the odds. It was a lesson in perseverance and dignity that resonated deeply with him.

Chapter 46

While he was still unpacking his boxes, meticulously adjusting each item to its place after his move, Tarakna was pondering the next steps in his ambitious plan. His thoughts were carefully compartmentalized by the acoustic vacuum in his helmet, a bubble of tranquility sheltered from the tumult outside. Suddenly, an insidious vibration shook this quietude. His connected watch was vibrating frantically. The anonymous call burst into his headset like a fire alarm piercing the hushed silence.

Without wasting a moment, he transferred the call and picked up, the aggressive noise forcing him to wince:

- Hello, sir, I'm the delivery man. I'm here to deliver your package.

- Hello, sir, I'll be right down. I'll be right down.

A broad smile, as mysterious as it was enigmatic, spread across Tarakna's face. He knew it was his machine, the computational beast he'd been waiting days for, that had finally arrived.

Downstairs, the deliveryman was about to roll his loaded cart up to the door of the house when Tarakna stopped him with a quick but confident gesture.

- No need, just leave it here, please. I'll take care of it.

The deliveryman, a little disconcerted by this unusual request, placed the parcel on his cart without asking any questions. He had Tarakna sign the delivery note before setting off again.

Tarakna gazed at his new acquisition with almost reverential admiration, like a conqueror observing a newly acquired treasure. He walked around the package, inspecting every angle with almost scientific precision. Then, with measured delicacy, he mounted the package on a dolly and headed for a small garage adjoining his home.

This garage, once used to house a small car, had been transformed by Tarakna into an air-conditioned room. He had called in a professional to install a powerful air-conditioning unit and seal all potential cold loss gaps. It was the ideal and necessary place to house the machine, especially in this region of southern Europe where forest fires raged and temperatures sometimes reached 45°C in the shade.

As soon as it was installed, the machine emitted a soft hum, indicating that it was in full operation. The screens installed by Tarakna in his living room, designed to supervise the entire system, flashed frantically, similar to the monitors in the control room of a giant infrastructure.

Tarakna stood in front of these screens for hours, scrutinizing every fluctuation. Training the clones for real-time operation was clearly progressing apace. Soon, he would be able to measure the quality of his new creation and determine any necessary adjustments.

Over the following days, Tarakna locked himself into an almost monastic routine, where every spare moment was devoted to observation and adjustment. He knew that perfection was not an option. Neglect of even the smallest detail could derail everything.

Chapter 47

Kenneth and Dihya took the elevator, no doubt for the last time, the metal doors closing softly behind them. The silence was interrupted only by the gentle hum of the car ascending to the upper floors. When they reached the top floor, they stepped out and took the narrow stairs leading to the Casa Delfino terrace. Their footsteps echoed softly in the early dawn, each echo seeming to mark the passage of time.

The light breeze from the Aegean made Dihya's hair dance, while the first rays of sunlight painted the horizon with a golden glow. Standing in front of the port of Chania, with the same breathtaking view stretching out before them, Kenneth turned to Dihya. His eyes, filled with emotion, met hers, and he tenderly took her in his arms for a long, passionate kiss.

"I promise to see you in Paris very soon," he murmured, his lips brushing Dihya's ear. It was a promise of unwavering sincerity, even if the digital detox program prevented Kenneth from accompanying her immediately. A few more days would separate them before their reunion, an eternity in their hearts.

In the distance, a cab honked, breaking the suspended moment between them. It was the signal, the irrevocable call to leave. Dihya, on the hotel's instructions, had asked for this cab to take her to the airport. It was parked in a narrow alley, right next to the hotel, ready to take her away from this place of romance and memories.

The two lovers quickly descended, their hearts heavy, to collect Dihya's luggage. Each step sounded like a hammer blow, marking the end of their idyllic stay. As they reached the cab, the separation became more tangible, more painful. With trembling hands, Kenneth gave Dihya's hand one last squeeze.

"I love you," he breathed, his words almost choked with emotion. Dihya, her eyes glistening with tears, replied with a sad but resolute smile.

As Dihya climbed into the cab, Kenneth felt a part of himself slipping away with her. The engine started, and the cab pulled away slowly, disappearing around the corner. Kenneth stood there, staring at the empty street where, just a few moments earlier, he was still holding the hand of the woman he loved.

The silence of the morning now embraced Chania, but in Kenneth's heart still echoed the soft murmur of their final farewell.

Chapter 48

Dihya returned to Paris after a memorable stay in Chania, her thoughts still imbued with memories of the island. On her return to the Herald, she discovered the paper's new premises. Formerly spread over three large floors of a Parisian building, the newspaper was now relegated to a single, small floor, albeit located in a more prestigious district. The mass redundancy of many colleagues, a direct consequence of the AI chatbot revolution, was a tangible reality that required adaptation and strength of character.

Dihya's eyes welled up with tears as she took in her new office. The loss of space and colleagues had created an oppressive void. As she struggled to keep her emotions in check, a familiar figure appeared in the distance. The director, whom she had rarely come across before her departure, also seemed transformed by time. Her magical stay in Chania had erased many memories, especially those she preferred to forget.

Now, in this small space, she would have to see the manager every day. He approached her, his face tinged with cold courtesy.

- Hello, Dihya, how are you? Did you have a good vacation?

- Hello Mr Gilbert, I'm fine thank you. My stay went very well.

- How do you like your new office?

- A bit sad, it has less neighbors now!

- That's life, you have to deal with it. It's either that or closure. We've chosen to keep the doors open.

- Open for a few, it's true, retorted Dihya.

- Count yourself lucky, you're one of them. Others weren't so lucky.

- Yes, luck.

Dihya turned to stare at her screen, letting the manager slip away. She knew the situation would be difficult, and so would living together under these new conditions. She wondered whether she would still have the freedom to tackle difficult subjects and conduct genuine investigations, or whether she would be relegated to producing insipid reports. This uncertainty weighed heavily on her mind. In the back of her mind, she sensed that, if the latter were the case, she wouldn't last long. The project of leaving journalism to open a farm would take shape for real in her thoughts, an escape from this disappointing reality.

As Dihya plunged into her reflections, memories of Chania flooded back, a stark contrast to the drab Parisian office. She recalled the sun-drenched beaches, the vibrant port and, above all, the freedom she had felt there. A freedom she feared she'd never find again in the narrow corridors and anonymous offices of the Herald.

But in the midst of these memories, one image stood out more vividly than the others: that of Kenneth. With his infectious laugh and sparkling eyes, he had made her stay even more memorable. They'd spent hours chatting, sharing their dreams and fears, and a special connection had formed between them. This chance meeting had turned into a deep relationship, and they had promised to see each other again soon. In a few days, Kenneth would be arriving in Paris, and the idea of meeting him again was one of the few rays of sunshine in this new, gloomy reality.

Yet somewhere inside her, a spark of determination was igniting. Dihya knew she had to fight for her journalistic integrity, for the stories that deserved to be told. She was ready to defy the restrictions imposed, to fight for every line of ink that would be printed. Because, deep down, journalism was more than a career to her, it was a vocation, a calling she couldn't ignore. Kenneth, the man she loved, had made that clear to her. The idea of seeing him again soon added a note of hope and optimism, strengthening her determination to make her voice heard in the tumult of change.

Chapter 49

Dihya's digital clone worked admirably when it came to speech, but the visual aspect left a lot to be desired. Artifacts and facial distortions were clearly visible when she spoke. Tarakna was in no way surprised; he'd expected this kind of result by now. He had already scoured the Internet for videos of Dihya, but despite the journalist's notoriety, he had found very few. Two or three interviews given by the investigative journalist following some of her investigations, nothing more. He needed much more to advance his plan. He knew that Dihya was back in Paris and that fed his ideas.

As he pondered his next move, his phone began to ring. It was Dihya calling Kenneth once again. Tarakna, on the lookout for any useful information, listened attentively to the conversation:

- Hello, hello Kenny.

- Hello, darling, thank you for calling.

- How are you?

- I can't wait for you to come back.

Kenneth sensed a slight fatigue in Dihya's voice and, naturally, wanted to make sure everything was okay.

- Are you sure you're okay? You look a little tired.

- Yes, I am. You're getting to know me.

- Nothing serious, I hope? asked Kenneth, worried.

- No, nothing bad. It's just that the atmosphere at work has become heavy. It's been a hard day. I feel like I'm in a cage, a prison.

- You gave me a fright. As far as work is concerned, it's not serious. I know it's hard without your old colleagues, but I'm sure you'll adapt quickly to the new conditions. This could even be an opportunity to forge new bonds. Remember, you're strong and you'll always be the Herald's Xena!

Dihya smiled at Kenneth's comforting words, all the more reason to hope to find him as soon as possible.

- I'm also calling to tell you that tonight I won't be able to stay up as usual. I'll need some time to research some items, as I'll be attending an important auction tomorrow.

- You, at an auction?

- Yes, I'll talk to you about it later.

- Don't worry, we'll do that. Before you hang up, do you need me to bring you anything from here?

- No, nothing special, thank you. Just don't forget the book I left you.

Dihya was very fond of the book on the island of Delos that she had bought at Athens airport. It contained unpublished information about her origins, which she didn't want to lose.

- Obviously, I won't forget. I'll bring back a little surprise anyway. I hope you like it.

- I'm sure I will. I've loved everything I've experienced with you so far, so there's no reason for that to change. Well, I'll leave you to it. Good evening and see you tomorrow.

- Thank you, darling. A big kiss. See you tomorrow.

Kenneth hung up and immediately set off in search of the promised surprise.

Chapter 50

The heated conversation with Dihya about her chain and Berber history a few days ago had planted an idea in Kenneth's mind. He wanted to please her with a bold gesture, especially for someone like him who had little enthusiasm for tattoos. But when you fall in love with a new culture, as he had, you push certain boundaries.

Night had fallen on the port of Chania, and darkness enveloped the town. Kenneth, reluctant to venture far from his hotel after dusk, contented himself with asking a few passers-by on the quayside if a good tattooist was working nearby. Each time, one name invariably came up: Tsiotsios. What's more, Tsiotsios owned a tattoo parlor, the Medusa Tattoo Studio, just a few hundred meters from Casa Delfino, a mere five-minute walk from the port. Without further ado, Kenneth set off.

When he arrived at his destination, Kenneth found himself in front of a discreet store, entirely glazed and framed in simple wood. Three large plant pots, placed on either side of the door, seemed to stand guard like sentinels watching over a sanctuary. He pushed open the door and uttered a "good morning" in his characteristic British accent. Tsiotsios and a customer, whose lower foot he adorned with an imposing tattoo, had already responded with a hearty "kalimera".

Kenneth was about to sit down to wait, but the tattooist called out to him in a rough tone:

- *We will close, sir. Last client here.*

Kenneth realized at once that the firm was closing and that he wouldn't be booked tonight. Disappointment overwhelmed him, especially as the night was drawing on and he was due to leave for Paris shortly. Determined not to give up, he tried one last explanation:

- I'm a tourist and I'm leaving tomorrow (Kenneth was actually leaving the day after tomorrow and lied to make Tsiotsios give in). I know you must be tired, but please make an exception.

- I'm sorry, I have to go.

- The tattoo I want is simple, I assure you, and it won't take you long, reiterated Kenneth.

Tsiotsios, after a moment's hesitation, gave in before Kenneth could continue his argument.

- OK, you'll have to wait a bit then. About an hour, until I finish with this customer.

- Of course, no problem. I'll wait as long as it takes.

Kenneth settled into a small wooden chair. Failing to surf the Internet on his phone, which he quickly put back in his pocket after mechanically taking it out, he spent his time observing the studio, scrutinizing every detail. The decor, at once sober and welcoming, was marked by framed works of art and objects that seemed to tell ancient stories.

Time was running out for Kenneth, but he had no choice but to wait.

Finally, it was his turn. Tsiotsios turned to him and asked what he wanted. Kenneth took out a small sheet of paper on which he had scribbled a symbol.

Tsiotsios smiled when he saw the leaf.

- Is that all you want? A letter? Kappa?

Kenneth knew it wasn't quite the Greek letter kappa, but it sure looked like it. He simply confirmed.

К

- Yes, that's right. It's simply the first letter of my first name, Kenneth.

- If you'd shown me this from the start, I'd have accepted without hesitation, added the tattoo artist. And where do you want it?

- On the arm, here.

- Okay, fine. Please sit down and don't move too much.

Kenneth removed his shirt before settling into the armchair. As soon as the needle grazed his skin, he felt a series of sharp tingles, like thousands of tiny needles piercing the surface. The pain was sharp, but bearable, evolving into a kind of vibration that ran down his arm. With each movement of the machine, he felt increasing heat under his skin, accompanied by a strange numbness. The sound of the machine, a constant electric hum, filled the room, oscillating in harmony with the artist's precise gestures. The sound, at once soothing and hypnotic, seemed to mark the rhythm of time, each modulation indicating a new advance in the work.

As the tattoo took shape, Kenneth lost himself in thought, contemplating the path that had brought him to this point. Memories of his conversations with Dihya, of the beauty of Chania, and of his desire to make this bold gesture blended into a vivid mosaic. Tsiotsios, focused and methodical, worked with admirable dexterity, each stroke of the needle reinforcing Kenneth's determination.

The monotonous repetition of the noise created an almost meditative atmosphere, where pain and sound merged into a unique experience. Kenneth closed his eyes, concentrating on the steady hum, each vibration becoming a reminder of the transformation taking place on his skin.

To take his mind off the pain, Tsiotsios finally struck up a conversation. He asked Kenneth what he had come to Chania to do. Rather talkative, it was he who finally monopolized the discussion, recounting his various activities.

George Tsiotsios was an artist of considerable experience and talent in body art. He specialized in custom designs, including classics, portraits and tribals. In the mid-90s, he and his colleague had founded the Stigma Skin Society in Athens, with the aim of promoting the art of tattooing and bringing tattoo artists together to exchange ideas and techniques. He organized the first International Tattoo Exhibition in Athens, a major event that attracted renowned artists from all over the world. Tsiotsios had traveled extensively and collaborated with many famous artists throughout Europe. In addition, George was a fervent animal rights activist and was actively involved in a movement to end violence and barbaric acts against animals in Crete.

Kenneth was almost awakened from a deep sleep when Tsiotsios announced that his tattoo was complete.

- That's it, I'm done. Take a look at the result and let me know what you think.

Kenneth straightened up to take a look at his arm. He felt a strange sensation as he discovered the indelible design that would henceforth be an integral part of his body. He was pleased with the result. The symbol was rather discreet, exactly what he wanted. Looking down at his arm, Kenneth felt a wave of pride and satisfaction wash over him. The symbol, though simple, represented much more than just a letter. It was a reminder of this very moment, this very place, and his magical encounter with Dihya.

- It's perfect. I like it. Thank you very much for this.

Tsiotsios nodded, pleased to have been able to meet his customer's modest request.

As Kenneth put his shirt back on, he knew he was taking with him an indelible souvenir of an unforgettable stay. He thanked Tsiotsios before taking out his phone to pay. As he moved his device closer to the payment terminal, he remembered that he couldn't do so, as the application required Internet access. He finally took out his credit card and paid without saying anything more. It was getting very late and he didn't feel like staying out too long. He left a small bill in his pocket as a tip before waving goodbye to Tsiotsios and leaving the office.

Kenneth strolled down the darkened streets of the port of Chania, thinking what his darling Dihya would think of his gesture. Would she be pleased, she who loved symbols so much?

It was with this doubt that he fell asleep that evening, awaiting his imminent departure for Paris.

Chapter 51

Dihya, just back in Paris, was informed of an imminent auction of an object that aroused a particular interest in her. Normally, she was neither an art collector nor an auction enthusiast, but this time the object in question was particularly close to her heart. She hoped to acquire it for 8,000 euros, although the actual value was unknown to her. However, she had set herself a maximum budget of 12,000 euros, an amount she considered reasonable. According to her meticulous Internet research, this type of object rarely exceeded 15,000 euros. She therefore considered her chances of purchase rather favorable.

The scene was the Hôtel Drouot, the sanctuary of Parisian auctions. As she entered, Dihya was immediately struck by the diversity of the crowd: knowledgeable collectors, passionate antique dealers, the curious and a few rare fellow journalists, all drawn by the announcement of the sale of a marble bust representing an ancient king.

The excitement in the room was palpable. Conversations were lively, animated by feverish speculation about the price the precious bust might fetch. The sales room was spacious and elegantly decorated, with a seating arrangement facing a dais where the auctioneer would soon take his place. At the center of all attention, the marble bust sat majestically on a pedestal, skilfully lit to emphasize its fine detail and venerable age. It was a representation of the Numidian king Juba II, wearing a taenia, a finely sculpted headband that added to the work's historical and aesthetic value.

Visitors streamed slowly into the large hall. Some were still leafing through the sale catalog, their fingers brushing the pages as if they contained buried secrets. Others murmured in low voices, exchanging hopes and strategies with a perceptible intensity. At the back of the room, a photographer, his large camera hanging heavily around his neck, stood ready, keen-eyed and pointed, to capture the crucial moment when the hammer would seal the fate of each lot.

With a delicate gesture, Dihya opened the catalog and scanned the lines, searching for the description of the coveted object. Her eyes ran over every word with feverish concentration, her mind soaking up every detail as if it might give her an edge in the impending auction battle.

===================================

Batch No. 150

Portrait of Juba II, King of Mauretania from 25 B.C. to 23 A.D. He is depicted as a young man, face turned to the right, beardless, mouth slightly ajar with full, sensual lips. The modelling of the flesh is idealized and characterizes the young sovereign's ethnicity. Beneath the high forehead, the arch of the eyebrow forms a shadowy area at the inner corner of the eye. His abundant hair, with its rebellious curls, is encircled by a wide royal headband tied at the back of his head, the sides of which fall down the nape of his neck. The torso is covered by the paludamentum stapled to the right shoulder. White marble. Late 1st century B.C. Height: 30 cm (34 cm with the stopper) Born around 52 B.C., Juba II was the son of Juba I. He was one of the captives in the Roman Empire. He was one of the captives in Caesar's triumph of 46 BC, and was raised in Italy and Numidia, receiving the kingdom of Mauretania when his father committed suicide. In the sixth year of his reign (19 BC), he married Cleopatra Selene II, daughter of the great Cleopatra and Marc Antony. Together, they formed one of the most refined courts in the Mediterranean. Coins bearing their effigies have been minted.

===================================

Dihya took out her phone and took a photo of the two coins illustrated. She looked at them very closely. Although the writing was Latin and the coins were a little weathered, she could clearly make out the two names, Juba and Cleopatra. Then she resumed her reading.

= =

His kingdom stretched from the Atlantic to Ampsaga (eastern Algeria), where he sought to introduce Greek and Roman culture. He acquired a great reputation in science and literature, and wrote numerous books in Greek, often quoted by Pliny the Elder. We owe him a treatise on euphorbia, a medicinal plant from the Atlas mountains, writings on Arabia, the Assyrians and a history of his ancestor Massinissa. He played an important role in the cultural exchanges resulting from his mixed heritage. He died in 23 CE, and was buried with Cleopatra Selene in a tomb near Tipasa now known as the "Tomb of the Christian". The portrait presented here, with its ample style and perceptible idealization, owes much to the Hellenistic sculptural tradition desired by Juba II.

Apart from a bronze bust exhibited in the Rabat museum and a damaged marble bust exhibited in the Louvre, all we knew of him was a certain profile, appearing on a few rare coins (see photos). This marble bust is therefore an exceptional object in every respect, and its lucky purchaser will have a rare pearl in his hands!

= =

As soon as she had finished reading the description, Dihya thought back to the Royal Mausoleum of Mauretania, or "Tomb of the Christian" as it is better known, which she had visited on more than one occasion. It was indeed attributed to Juba II, but certain archaeological studies on the mausoleum's architecture placed it at a period prior to Roman domination of North Africa. It would appear to be an indigenous, Berber construction, simply covered with a Greek shirt many years later.

Dihya's thoughts were suddenly interrupted by the appearance of the auctioneer, who stepped up to the podium and adjusted his microphone. A respectful silence ensued as excitement mounted. He began with a detailed description of the bust, highlighting its historical and artistic importance. Every detail seemed to captivate the audience, from the king's Numidian origins to the exceptional quality of the marble used.

The bidding began. The first bids were quickly placed, and tension mounted as the amounts climbed. Bidders, strategically dispersed around the room, discreetly raised their pallets or waved to the auctioneer. The atmosphere was electrifying, with each new bid triggering murmurs and exchanged glances.

Dihya didn't even have the opportunity to wave her hand to bid. Her maximum budget of 12,000 euros was far exceeded at the opening bid. The amounts went up at a dizzying pace: 650,000 then 700,000 then 750,000 then 800,000. Dihya was stunned. She hadn't expected such a frenzy around this bust. Was Juba II a star in a parallel world she didn't know existed? A real mystery settled in her mind.

After a series of impassioned proposals, the price reached a peak: 900,000 euros now! Everyone in the room looked at each other. Where would it all end? The auctioneer was waiting for a sign from the audience and, just as he raised the hammer, a discreet hand from a gentleman sitting off to the side of the room beckoned. The auctioneer raised the hammer to 920,000 and made a series of calls to the room. After a moment of suspense, a lady nodded. A new bid fell.

The auctioneer, hammer in hand, scanned the room one last time before announcing the final price: 940,000 euros! The hammer fell with a thump, sealing the sale of the bust to an apparently French collector. Applause broke out, and the lucky buyer was congratulated by his peers.

Dihya moved towards the buyer to try and find out a little more about him, but he had quickly slipped away. He obviously wished to remain anonymous.

As Dihya left the room, she thought about how much the 30 cm-high bust of a Numidian king had cost - over a million euros, all expenses paid! She was both proud and bitter. This bust would enrich a private collection, instead of a museum, and put a slightly thicker veil over the history of the Berbers...

And the historical deepfake would thicken even more.

Chapter 52

Dihya was on her way home, twilight tinting the sky with an orange glow. As usual, she stopped by the letterbox to check the mail. That day, two envelopes were patiently awaiting her attention. One, small and plain, bore the logo of her bank. The other, larger and slightly thicker, immediately caught her eye. Intrigued by the handwriting and exotic stamp, she opened the envelope on the doorstep, unable to contain her curiosity.

Inside, bubble wrap revealed a small object: a glittery pink heart-shaped USB stick. A smile played across her lips; she was used to this kind of delivery. As an investigative journalist, whistle-blowers often used these devices to transmit sensitive information to her. But this glittering heart seemed to promise something even more singular.

A folded piece of paper accompanied the key. The message scrawled on it was clear and unequivocal:

> *Kompromat in high places !*

Dihya's heart raced. She immediately realized that it was probably a compromising video involving a prominent political figure. Her hands trembled slightly as she rushed inside, her bag abandoned at the entrance.

She went straight to her desk, her heart beating wildly.

Her journalistic instincts told her to follow strict procedure: wait until the following day to go to the Herald to scan the key on a dedicated machine, isolated from the newspaper's network, to avoid any risk of a potentially devastating virus. But excitement outweighed reason.

With a feverish gesture, she plugged the USB key into her personal computer. A popup immediately appeared, revealing a single file named "PM_Kompromat.mp4". Dihya stared at the screen, her mind racing. "PM? Prime Minister? It was the most obvious hypothesis, but she couldn't be sure.

She double-clicked on the file, her palms sweaty with anticipation. On the first try, nothing happened. Her fingers were trembling so much that she could barely control the mouse.

Finally, the video started up. The image was blurred at first, but soon became clear. What she saw stopped her in her tracks.

Chapter 53

As she stood there, staring at her screen and pondering her next move, Dihya's phone suddenly rang, interrupting her train of thought. It was a text message from Kenneth, accompanied by a close-up photo of his arm. The image revealed a very recent tattoo, representing a letter.

Dihya couldn't help but crack a smile, albeit a tense one, when she saw the photo. The tattoo had a double meaning: the initial of Kenneth's first name in Berber and also that of her own nickname, Kahina. This strong symbol would undoubtedly strengthen the budding bond between them. Dihya's heart warmed at the thought, a mixture of pride and tenderness washing over her.

She planned to call Kenneth, as she did almost every night, to discuss the tattoo and tell him about her day, including the incredible auction she'd attended. However, her mind was elsewhere. The kompromat in her hands was shattering all her certainties. It weighed heavily on her shoulders, darkening her mood.

Dihya replied with a brief text message:

It's daring. You're incredible!
We'll talk later. I love you.

She put down her phone and sank back into her armchair, her mind swirling with contradictory thoughts. This kompromat could change the course of her life, and potentially that of those around her.

Her phone vibrated again. A message from Kenneth:

*I can't wait to tell you all about it.
And you, how was your day?*

Dihya hesitated, her fingers hovering over the keyboard. Should she share her burden with Kenneth? Should she plunge him into this turmoil? Part of her desperately wanted to trust him, but the other feared the consequences.

Finally, she replied:

Intense day. Lots to tell you. Can't wait to see you.

Dihya knew she had to make a decision quickly. She took a deep breath, stood up and made her way to the window. The view of the City of Light reminded her of the many intrigues brewing in the shadows. She clutched the USB key tightly in her hand, determined to find the best way to deal with this complex situation.

Chapter 54

Dihya felt a wave of triumph mixed with horror. This scoop could be a game-changer, not only for her career, but for the whole country. Her mind bubbled with a thousand questions. Who had sent her that video? Why now? And above all, how was she going to handle this explosive information without putting her own life in danger? The choice she made in the next few hours could well decide the fate of the entire nation. The weight of this responsibility fell on her shoulders.

Dihya stood trembling in front of her window, watching the streets of Paris below. In her hands, she held a media bomb capable of blowing up the government with a single click. The suit affair that had brought down former French Prime Minister François Fillon, and paved the way for Macron in the 2017 French presidential elections, seemed trivial in comparison to what she held.

The video lasted just three minutes, but every second seemed interminable. It showed the Prime Minister in the company of a young woman in her thirties. Their arrival at the hotel was filmed, followed by scenes in a room where, for a self-proclaimed defender of conservative values, married with four children, this video would undoubtedly sign his political death. Worse still, a rail of cocaine spread across the table added to the horror of the scandal. It didn't matter if it was what it looked like, social networks would seize on it and doubt would be sown everywhere, irreparably destroying his career.

Dihya was faced with a dilemma. If she revealed the information, the country could be saved, but her own career would undoubtedly suffer. If she kept it to herself, she would be betraying her duty as a journalist and putting the country at risk. Using a kompromat to put pressure on a politician was a classic.

She had to inform the Herald's publications director, but not by telephone. From experience, she knew that investigative journalists were often under surveillance. It was getting late, but she hurried to the paper's offices. The director, who was often there late at night, must still be there. She called him to make sure, and he confirmed his presence. She asked him to wait for her, just in case he was about to leave.

Dihya jumped into her car and sped off down the streets of Paris. As she sped off, a thousand scenarios played out in her mind. She thought about the director's reaction, the media storm that would follow, and her own safety. The headlights of the cars passing her flashed like so many alerts, and each red light seemed like an eternity.

Arriving at the Herald, she leapt out of the car and ran towards the main entrance. The director was waiting for her, looking grave and aware of the urgency of the situation.

Chapter 55

Together, Dihya and the director watched the kompromat video over and over again, each passage reinforcing the magnitude of the potential scandal. The bluish light from the screen illuminated their tense faces, making each shadow deeper. Dihya could feel the adrenaline pumping, while the director, his forehead beaded with sweat, measured the gravity of the situation.

The director, usually such a self-confident man, was livid. Aware that his career was in danger of being shattered, he adopted a cautious tone.

- We need to verify the authenticity of this video, he murmured, his eyes still riveted to the screen. If it's true, it will turn the whole political field upside down.

Dihya, biting her lower lip, knew how explosive this revelation could be.

- You know very well that in little Paris, rumors have been circulating for a long time about a hidden relationship between the Prime Minister and this assistant, she said, her words as sharp as shards of glass.

- Yes, I know that, but we need to be sure of its authenticity. Let me remind you that we are 72 hours away from the presidential elections, and the PM is widely considered to be the favorite. If this video were to come out, it would be the end for him.

The manager paused, as if assessing the weight of his own words. Dihya pressed him.

- That's just it, we're running out of time. If it's going to come out, it's going to come out now. We've only got 24 hours left.

France was entering a period of "media silence", when all electioneering was forbidden. This moment of imposed calm, though necessary, made their task all the more pressing.

The manager shook his head, fighting the palpable urgency.

- But no, we don't have enough time to authenticate it and cross-check it with other sources. Suppose it's a *fake* and we discover it after the fact. We wouldn't even have time to issue a denial because of the reserve period. It would be a real mess. Not only would no one believe us, but we'd even be accused of trying to backtrack to protect the PM.

Dihya clenched her fists, her frustration bursting out in words.

- But you can see that this video is authentic, she argued. There are no artifacts or other clues to suggest that it's been edited.

- Yes, but I prefer to err on the side of caution. The stakes are too high. Besides, it's the PM's private life - he's got the right to screw whoever he wants!

Dihya burst out, her patience wearing thin.

- The PM spends his time giving lessons in virtue and moralizing to everyone, she snapped. He deserves to be taken off his pedestal, doesn't he?

The director stared at her, his eyes burning with cold determination.

- The elections are coming up, and it's up to the French people to decide whether or not to vote for him, not us. We're here to inform, not influence votes. The debate is over.

Dihya laughed inwardly, a bitter, yellow laugh. She understood the call for caution, but to speak of impartiality at this stage seemed ridiculous. The media had long since abandoned their role as informers and become sounding boards for certain opinions.

The director, judging the risks too great for him and his newspaper, refused to publish the information. Dejected, Dihya left the office. As she drove through Paris in the dark of night, a thought occurred to her. What if she passed on the kompromat to colleagues at another media outlet?

As she made her way through the dark alleys, she remembered some trusted contacts, freelance journalists willing to brave storms for a good story. These thoughts swirled in her mind, fueling her energy and determination.

Eyes glued to the road, she let go of the steering wheel with one hand to switch on her phone and request a call.

- Siri, call Peoni.

The bell rang for the second time and Dihya's heart was beating a thousand miles an hour. Peoni was an old comrade, a fearless journalist with a keen sense of justice and an insatiable thirst for truth. No doubt he'd get the story out if he could cross-check it with other sources.

Dihya took a deep breath, aware that the next few seconds could be decisive for the future of an entire country.

Chapter 56

Peoni, Dihya's journalist colleague, finally picked up the call after the third ring.

- Hi, Dihya, how are you? How are you doing?

Peoni's familiar voice echoed in Dihya's ear, but her mind was elsewhere, tormented by a dull, inarticulate anguish. As if an invisible hand had slapped her awake, she suddenly pulled herself together.

- Hi, Peoni, I'm sorry. I mispronounced a friend's name a bit and it ended up on you. Siri takes us at our word, as you know! Sorry to have bothered you.

- OK, no worries. Have a nice evening.

- Thank you, Peoni, you too. See you soon.

Dihya hung up, her heart pounding. She didn't know what had just happened, but her unfailing instinct was to turn back. Unfortunately, some of the damage had already been done. The moment she had opened the video file on her personal computer, malware had installed itself. The video, a trap cleverly orchestrated by Tarakna, allowed the latter to break into her devices and steal her personal data.

For once, the Herald's publications director, by refusing to publish the kompromat information and covering it up, had done Dihya a huge favor. Without this decision, Dihya would have been plunged into an inextricable mess.

Back at home, Dihya couldn't help but look at the kompromat once more. She scrutinized every image, every detail, looking for manipulation, but nothing jumped out at her. The idea of sending it to a friend specializing in video editing crossed her mind for a moment, but she quickly gave up. The subject was too serious to be entrusted to anyone, even someone she trusted.

The minutes ticked by, her thoughts swirling around the discussion with the manager, her eyes glued to the screen. Finally, she turned off the computer and headed for the bathroom. As she emerged, ready to collapse on the sofa, a ding sounded on her phone. A text message had just arrived:

Good evening darling, expected arrival tomorrow at 6:45pm, CDG, T2F, Flight AF9013. See you soon. Love you!

Dihya smiled in spite of herself. She had almost forgotten that Kenneth would be arriving tomorrow. The thought comforted her for a moment, a breath of fresh air in the midst of the storm raging in her mind. She should go and wait for him at the airport, but for now, she let herself fall onto the sofa. As soon as she had spread out, Dihya fell asleep, her heavy eyelids finally relieved by rest. Tomorrow would be another day, with its challenges and hopes. But tonight she could at least find some semblance of peace.

Chapter 57

Tarakna had pulled out all the stops to make his kompromat credible. Aware that the Prime Minister would be spending a night in the provinces as part of his election campaign, he had meticulously organized his plan. He had managed to obtain the address of the hotel where the head of government was to stay. His assistant, inseparable from him, was staying in the same hotel, albeit on a different floor.

For Tarakna, it was essential to mix authenticity with deception to make his deepfake irrefutable. On the day of the Prime Minister's visit, he stationed himself at a safe distance from the hotel and filmed his arrival with his assistant. This first extract, visible at the beginning of the kompromat, was indeed authentic. The rest, on the other hand, was an illusion.

Tarakna himself had rented a room in this hotel for the same night. After the evening meeting, he discreetly followed the Prime Minister to his room. The bodyguards, watching over the politician's safety, prevented him from getting too close, but it was enough for him to note the exact location. The next day, on leaving the hotel, Tarakna asked to extend his stay by one night, specifying that he wanted a room on the third floor, overlooking the public garden. Luckily, or rather provocatively, the only room meeting his criteria was the one occupied by the Prime Minister.

That evening, Tarakna brought a prostitute into the room. A miniature camera, hidden behind the ventilation grid, recorded everything. The rest was child's play for him, an expert in artificial intelligence. The numerous images and videos of the Prime Minister and his assistant readily available on the Internet had made the task much easier. He easily transferred the silhouettes of the politician and his assistant onto the video using the *swapping* technique. The result was perfect.

Juxtaposed with the real video of the Prime Minister's arrival at the hotel, the whole thing looked totally authentic. Tarakna was hoping to strike a blow. Not only did he intend to use this video to infiltrate Dihya's devices and retrieve her data, but he also hoped that if the rumors of an adulterous relationship between the Prime Minister and his assistant were true, this video would be perceived by the public as irrefutable proof.

Worse still, if, like many politicians, the Prime Minister and his assistant were under the influence of alcohol or drugs, they could themselves be fooled by the video. Drunk or drugged people rarely remember the events of the previous night. Watching the video, they might believe it to be a clandestine recording, even if it never took place.

Tarakna called this process "deeptake", a video intended to recreate an event not actually recorded. It's a kind of journey into the past to film a scene, real or fictional, then return to the present with the recording in hand.

Tarakna, who was passionate about psychology and had devoured hundreds of studies in the field, knew that even without the effect of any substance, it is possible to create in the human brain what is known as "false memories" or "false memory syndrome". Sometimes, all it takes is showing a person fictitious images or videos of themselves to make them believe they have actually experienced what is depicted. "A picture is worth a thousand lies", said one such study.

By performing the *deeptake* feat, Tarakna knew he had the new *sextape* blackmail method, ready to be used by criminals in the near future, if it wasn't already the case.

To blackmail a human with fake, you should have thought of that!

Chapter 58

Night had fallen, shrouding the sky in an oppressive darkness. Dihya, nervous, was driving to Charles de Gaulle airport for the first time. She had never driven there before, but the special occasion of meeting up with Kenneth, her lover, made the adventure worthwhile. Navigating the various terminals and finding the entrance to the parking lot near terminal 2F proved a daunting task, but after many detours, she finally made it.

She took the elevator to the arrivals level and walked over to a display screen. It was 7 p.m., and Kenneth should have landed fifteen minutes ago. He should be in the baggage reclaim area, but his plane was twenty minutes late.

Dihya waited, her mind wandering to the joy of reuniting with Kenneth and the warmth of his arms. The last few days without him had been trying, especially after the turbulence in her work as an investigative journalist. Her thoughts were interrupted by an advertisement on a billboard:

"Give your Tesla freedom and let it escape".

Tesla, always at the forefront of AI technology, was well ahead of Uber in the rental of autonomous cabs, but faced fierce competition from the many Chinese suppliers well established in the market. Tesla, which had always refused to advertise its vehicles, was forced to change its strategy. With a wide range of advertisements, it now encouraged individuals to make the most of their unused vehicles, rather than letting them sit in the garage.

Dihya, about to switch on her phone to check the time, saw her screen light up with a message:

Arrived. See you soon ☺

A smile lit up her face. Kenneth was safe and sound, and finding him was only a matter of minutes. She positioned herself by the sliding door through which passengers exited into the arrivals hall, hoping to be the first to see her beloved.

The minutes ticked by, the waves of passengers came and went, but there was no sign of Kenneth. After twenty minutes, anxiety began to creep over her. She tried to call him, but only the voicemail answered. Panic began to take hold of her, each unanswered ring fuelling her fears. She was about to head for the information point when a new message arrived:

I'm under arrest. Call my lawyer Robert Hanfman.

Dihya's world collapsed. She tried frantically to call Kenneth back, but his phone was now switched off. Sitting on a bench, she held her face in her hands, reality bearing down heavily on her. The days ahead were shaping up to be a nightmare. But she knew she had to act.

- Siri, call the office of Robert Hanfman.

Siri quickly found the number of the famous lawyer's office on the Internet, and the call was transferred to a colleague on duty.

- Hello, I'm Mister Simon Cartier from the Hanfman law firm. How can I help you?

- Hello sir, I'm Dihya, a friend of Kenneth Lewis, one of Robert Hanfman's clients. He was arrested on his return from a trip and asked me to contact you.

- Don't worry, Madame, replied Simon in a reassuring voice. I'll inform Robert immediately.

Chapter 59

Kenneth's shadow hung over the passenger seat like a ghostly presence, a heavy absence weighing on Dihya. He should have been there, by her side, but fate had decided otherwise. Kenneth would now find himself in a cell in a Paris police station, or worse, behind bars in a prison.

Dihya's tears blurred her vision. The road ahead became an indistinct blur, and she had to keep wiping her eyes to see clearly. Questions swirled in her mind, plunging her into total confusion. What was Kenneth accused of? Had he hidden such serious things from her?

Arriving home, exhausted and distraught, Dihya collapsed on her sofa. The slightest effort to eat seemed insurmountable, and sleep stubbornly eluded her. All night long, she replayed her memories, her moments with Kenneth, searching for clues in the past that might explain the nightmarish present.

With the first light of dawn, her eyes swollen and red from lack of sleep, Dihya headed for Hanfman's office. Each step echoed through the corridors of the imposing building, amplifying her anxiety. After a long wait in the waiting room, she finally learned that Kenneth had been transferred to the Santé prison in Paris. The lawyer, trying to reassure her, promised to do all he could to get him out of this hellhole. However, Hanfman was evasive about the reasons for his incarceration, preferring to let Kenneth explain the situation himself.

The only bright spot in this gloomy affair was the modernity of the Santé prison. Dihya learned that prisoners had had access to a telephone for years and, more recently, to the Internet on a limited basis, thus facilitating their reintegration. In the event of a health crisis, they could also benefit from "virtual visits" via Skype, allowing two hours of daily communication with their loved ones. This was a late step forward in France, compared with other countries that adopted this system as early as the 2019 Covid crisis.

But what Dihya didn't know was that Tarakna, the shadow lurking behind this plot, had anticipated everything. Every call she made, every message she sent, would be intercepted. Her phone was under constant surveillance, and Tarakna was waiting, ready to carry out his diabolical plan.

Chapter 60

Dihya quickly applied to the prison administration at La Santé for permission to visit. She knew it would take a few days, even weeks. Virtual visits, on the other hand, were much less risky and took two to three days to be approved. She therefore hoped for a call from Kenneth at any time, provided he was able to pass on her name from his list of visitors to the prison administration. But after the events of the last few hours, she doubted everything.

At work, nothing was going right. Dihya had neither the energy nor the concentration to investigate or write articles for the Herald. She made a brief appearance at the paper's offices, but, lost in thought, didn't even notice a colleague's greeting. Finally, she took a two-week sick leave, prescribed by her doctor for severe depression.

At home, she was running around in circles, not knowing what to do. Her heart was pounding with every ring of the phone. The false alarms were piling up, and her frustration was growing. Doubt also crept in: what if Kenneth wasn't who she thought he was? Could she have fallen in love with a man capable of the worst horrors?

In search of answers, she scoured the Internet, looking for the slightest clue about Kenneth. Just then, her phone rang, shattering the room's heavy silence. The number was blocked, so it could have been anyone. She hurriedly picked it up.

- Hello, good morning.

- Hi, Dihya, it's Kenneth.

- Oh, my God, Kenny, how are you?

- I'm fine, don't worry. I'm hanging in there.

- But why did you take so long to call me? I was worried sick.

- It wasn't up to me. I had to wait for permission from the authorities. I've just received it. You're the first person I call.

- That's all right. But what exactly are you accused of?

Kenneth took a deep breath. The story he was about to tell seemed so unreal, even to him.

- I'm accused of premeditated murder of a young woman in my office.

Dihya was speechless for a moment, before catching her breath and taking a big gulp of air.

- What is it? Murder? But you weren't even there. You've been away from Paris for a month!

- Yes, but what I'm accused of happened before I left.

- I don't know what you're talking about. Have you ever been worried about this business before you left?

- Yes, I was placed in police custody before being released, pending further investigation.

Dihya suddenly realized that Kenneth had kept the whole thing from her, and a big doubt crept into her mind as to his sincerity. She remained silent, digesting what she had just heard.

One thing was certain: the next few days would be tough. Whatever happened, she'd have to be strong, she told herself. Just hold on.

Tarakna, lurking in the shadows, listened to every word, every sound of the conversation. A satisfied smile spread across his face. His plan was unfolding exactly as he had imagined, without the slightest hitch.

Chapter 61

After this initial brief telephone discussion, Kenneth suggested that Dihya switch to a video call via Skype. Dihya had been dreading this moment, and her heart began to beat frantically as she waited for the image to appear.

The connection took a few moments to stabilize, and finally Kenneth's face appeared on the screen. Dihya was taken aback by the scene unfolding before her eyes. Kenneth, the athletic man who had embraced her so vigorously a few days earlier, suddenly seemed to have aged ten years. His features, once full of life, were now marked by a profound sadness. He was wearing a prison straitjacket, a garb she'd only seen in horror movies.

The background of the cell was dark, the walls bare and narrow, lending a claustrophobic atmosphere to the scene. Muffled noises and screams continually disrupted their discussion, adding to the sinister atmosphere of the moment.

Dihya was eager to hear Kenneth's account of the circumstances surrounding his arrest. Her curiosity was all-consuming, and she wanted to understand every detail of this strange and disturbing story. Kenneth began his account, tracing the events from the beginning to that fateful moment when he was arrested on his return from his trip. Dihya pressed him with questions, her eyes shining with concern and confusion.

- Yes, but why didn't you tell me sooner? she asked, her hands trembling.

- What do you want me to say? That I've been accused of murder when I've only known you for a few days? replied Kenneth, his face twitching in anguish.

- Yes, we told each other everything, you didn't have to hide anything from me, she insisted, her tears threatening to fall.

Kenneth sighed deeply before replying:

- To be honest, I was afraid it would scare you into ending our relationship. Besides, I know I'm innocent. I didn't expect to be arrested like this.

Dihya didn't want to burden Kenneth any further. Despite her inner turmoil, she sought to reassure him of her unwavering support.

- I'm here for you, Kenneth. I won't let you down, she said softly.

Their eyes met through the screen, and despite the distance and the circumstances, an invisible bond seemed to unite them more than ever. Their conversation lasted for a few more moments, the words becoming fewer and fewer, before the connection was abruptly severed. The two hours had flown by at dizzying speed, leaving Dihya alone with her thoughts, determined to discover the truth and help Kenneth out of this nightmare.

Chapter 62

Tarakna's diabolical plan was entering its final phase. Kenneth and Dihya's clones had been ready for several days, but Dihya's clone still lacked a crucial ingredient to achieve its ultimate goal. Tarakna wanted to endow this clone with subliminal psychological manipulation capabilities, a method of remote torture. This is unprecedented.

Tarakna had immersed himself in the "torture manuals" used by the CIA, seven massive documents declassified in the 1990s thanks to a Freedom of Information Act request filed by The Baltimore Sun. These manuals, replete with psychological torture techniques, were the key to his plan.

Conversational agents, such as ChatGPT, are AI models capable of assimilating specific knowledge to enhance their skills. By feeding them additional databases, they can provide precise, relevant answers. Similarly, Tarakna had instructed Dihya's clone, christened Kubark, to read the CIA's seven manuals and extract the best methods of psychological torture, adapting them for remote use via communications such as videoconferencing.

"Read the seven manuals and extract the best methods of psychological torture. Adapt these techniques so that they can be used at a distance, via communication such as videoconferencing. Keep it subtle so as not to arouse the target's suspicions."

Simultaneously, Tarakna programmed Kenneth's clone, nicknamed Lasso, to adopt a constantly optimistic and reassuring tone when addressing Dihya:

"Whatever the circumstances, adopt an optimistic tone and reassure your interviewer. Tell her how you're holding up and show her that you're in high spirits."

Thus, Lasso had to reassure Dihya about his condition, while in reality, the real Kenneth would be in the grip of the psychological torture inflicted by Kubark.

Tarakna, meticulous as ever, tested these techniques in advance. He was amazed by the results, which exceeded his expectations. A doubt even crept into his mind. Should he go through with this monstrous plan or turn back?

Chapter 63

As he did every day, Kenneth called Dihya via Skype to give her an update. He, a lawyer by profession, was closely following the progress of the legal proceedings and her defense orchestrated by sir Hanfman. He spoke to her in detail, hoping that, as a journalist, she would be able to publicize his story and help him out.

- Hello Dihya,

- Hello, Kenny, how are you today?

- It's getting better and better. I'm adapting and trying to keep as busy as possible.

- That's fine. Keep your spirits up and your mind occupied. I imagine you have access to a library, but don't hesitate if you don't find a book you'd like to read. I'll bring it to you.

- Thank you, Dihya, your support really helps me keep going.

- You're welcome.

After the words of encouragement and comfort, Dihya got to the heart of the matter, to understand a little more about the crime in Kenneth's office. The latter was constantly proclaiming his innocence and his total lack of understanding of what had happened. When Dihya asked him about the recording in the hands of the police, which was damning him, his answer remained the same: "I don't know what it is. I'm not crazy, I didn't do it". Dihya pushed him a little, not to overwhelm him, but to understand him better.

- If it were a fake recording, the police would have seen it immediately. And it didn't come from nowhere either, that's what the surveillance camera recorded. Surely she didn't invent it herself ex nihilo?

Kenneth knew Dihya was right, and that explained why he found himself in a cell. His answer, always the same, "I don't know", wasn't convincing, not even to his lover. And he could see it.

Doubt began to creep into Kenneth's mind and he began to doubt himself. What if he'd lost his head for a moment and done the irreparable without remembering?

Fragile in the situation he found himself in, Kenneth didn't rule out this hypothesis. So he did some research on the Internet to find out whether this was a possible phenomenon or not. And he who seeks often finds. He came across a disorder called "dissociative amnesia", a loss of memory due to psychological trauma rather than a physical cause. His would be of the "localized" type, since it would only concern this particular event. Perhaps he had suffered a psychological shock, the effect of which was felt long after his ex-wife had announced her divorce?

As Kenneth brought his hand up to his face to wipe his sweaty forehead, the tattoo he'd got in Crete appeared for the first time in Dihya's eyes. They hadn't talked about it until then, recent events having turned everything upside down. Dihya gave a tense smile, torn between joy at seeing this symbol and sadness at seeing her darling's situation.

- Why are you smiling? Do I look ridiculous in my Hannibal Lecter outfit? asked Kenneth, a little mockingly.

- No, I just saw your tattoo for the first time in real life. Sorry, I couldn't help but grimace.

- But no, don't worry. I know what you mean. This symbol means so much to both of us, at least to me. I hope you like it at least.

- Of course I like it. I just wish I could see it for real, touch it. But I will, sooner or later. Don't worry.

Kenneth took a deep breath, sadness still in his face. So much regret and disillusionment after the happy interlude he had spent with Dihya on the island of Crete.

Over the next few days, exchanges between Kenneth and Dihya became a little tense. The pressure of the investigation, the doubt that was creeping into Kenneth's mind, and above all the invisible Tarakna in ambush, were undermining his morale. He was battling inner demons and an outer one. The prospect of dissociative amnesia haunted him more than ever. What if he really was responsible? Each day in prison brought him a little closer to madness.

Chapter 64

Despite a growing sense of doubt that threatened to overwhelm him, Tarakna persisted with iron determination. His meticulously conceived plan required precise adjustments to maximize Kubark's psychological impact. The fateful moment had finally arrived.

Tarakna intensified his experiments, refining every detail. Kubark, having ingested the contents of the CIA manuals, had identified several torture techniques which he applied with formidable effectiveness in his communications with Kenneth. Among these strategies, subliminal sensory saturation proved particularly perverse. The clone would broadcast shrill, almost inaudible sounds, such as whistling or screaming, during their conversations. To each of Kenneth's complaints, Kubark would retort that it was all an illusion, a figment of his imagination, implanting the idea of madness in Kenneth's tormented mind.

While making adjustments to the clone, Tarakna remembered the famous Agassi strategy he had already tried out. He adapted it for Kubark, ordering his AI:

"Apply the Agassi strategy to detect your interviewer's moments of hesitation and attack him at the right moment. With every sign of hope he shows, you undermine his morale. Do it subtly so that it's not noticeable."

To avoid confusion with any sporting strategy, Tarakna explained to the clone the technique revealed by Andre Agassi. As a reminder, Agassi had discovered a tic in Boris Becker that enabled him to predict which way Becker would serve, giving him a considerable strategic advantage.

The last technique adopted by Tarakna, just as formidable as the previous ones, consisted in randomly activating Kubark and Lasso, on average every other time. This alternation created total confusion, with conversations between Dihya and Kenneth sometimes real, but not always. This uncertainty undermined Kenneth even more, as the fluctuation between Dihya's optimism and Kubark's destructive pessimism plunged him into a state of growing despair.

It's well known in psychology that fluctuations between optimism and despair can dramatically affect morale, creating emotional instability, disorientation and mental fatigue. This instability made it impossible for Kenneth to maintain a constant motivation to cope. Moments of hope were quickly undermined by negative thoughts, while prolonged emotional stress had deleterious physical effects on him, such as sleep disturbances and headaches. Even his immune system was at its weakest.

This emotional yo-yo, orchestrated by Tarakna, was gradually but inexorably destroying Kenneth's morale. Meanwhile, Dihya, oblivious to the plot, continued to be reassured by the other clone, Lasso, unaware of Kenneth's real ordeal.

Tarakna, who saw all that was going on like a god above men, knew that Kenneth wouldn't be able to cope indefinitely with this relentless erosion of his spirit. Each day, each conversation, brought him a little closer to total collapse, which would inevitably lead to committal to a psychiatric hospital. Tarakna, the undisputed master of manipulation, would triumph. His plan would have gone off without a hitch from start to finish. Unless, that is, a careless detail derailed everything.

Chapter 65

Kenneth was so used to hearing strange noises during his Skype conversations that his brain ended up imagining them even during real communication with Dihya. In the evenings, he would often listen to their recorded conversations again, trying to find comfort in Dihya's voice. But these recordings, imbued with strident sounds inserted by Kubark, only precipitated his descent into madness. For her part, Dihya, also recording their exchanges, did not suffer these disturbances, as Tarakna was not directly targeting her.

One evening, while they were chatting as usual, Dihya noticed something strange.

- Say Kenny, I don't see your tattoo.

- Yes, it is. Have a look.

Lasso held out his arm to show the tattoo, but Dihya still couldn't see the letter.

- No, I don't see anything. Did you take it off?

- No, I didn't erase it. It's there. It must be a problem with the lighting or a disturbance in the video stream.

Dihya, anxious not to add to Kenneth's anguish, changed the subject.

The tattoo was not visible on Kenneth's clone, as Tarakna did not have sufficient video data showing Kenneth with this mark. The only photo available was a close-up image sent by SMS to Dihya, insufficient to show the clone with the tattoo.

Lasso was very advanced, but not enough to be able to autonomously change its own appearance in real time. The AI needed to have a feedback loop on the image it was sending back to be able to change it at will. Tarakna was working on this feature, but it would still be a few months before it was operational.

Apart from this detail, the clone was almost perfect. With access to both conversations in parallel, Tarakna made sure that Kubark and Lasso never contradicted the actual exchanges between Dihya and Kenneth. When certain things seemed strange, Dihya put it down to Kenneth's fatigue. But the absence of the tattoo continued to haunt her. Why would Kenneth choose to erase it? What if he was lying about other things?

The next day, as soon as their Skype conversation began, Dihya broached the subject directly.

- Can you show me your tattoo, please?

Kenneth, exhausted and surprised by this unusual request, stretched out his arm towards the camera. The tattoo of the letter kappa was clearly visible.

- It's strange, yesterday I couldn't see it, retorted a surprised Dihya.

- Don't worry, I didn't erase it. It'll always be on me, I promise.

Words were hard to get out of Kenneth's mouth. With this parenthesis closed, Dihya became increasingly concerned about Kenneth's health, which seemed to be fluctuating. So, she returned to a more important subject, the legal proceedings and the impending trial.

- Kenny, where are we with the trial? Have you heard from sir Hanfman?

Kenneth hesitated, his thoughts clouded by the constant confusion between his conversations with Dihya and Kubark's manipulations.

- Yes, the lawyer tells me there are positive developments. We should have a hearing in a few weeks.

Dihya nodded, but she couldn't shake the feeling that something was wrong.

Chapter 66

Tarakna, lurking in the shadows of his lair, observed everything. His piercing eyes scrutinized every reaction on his supervision screens, capturing every micro-expression, every twitch. Tension mounted, each interaction a delicate dance between hope and despair. As the days passed, the cumulative effect of the psychological manipulations was seriously eroding Kenneth's mind. Dihya, for her part, seemed increasingly troubled, her instincts whispering that something was wrong.

Kubark, now the undisputed master of manipulation techniques, launched assault after assault at superhuman speed. Communication between Dihya and Kenneth became a veritable mental battlefield, a cognitive war orchestrated by Tarakna. Kubark subtly inserted suggestions and doubts into Kenneth's mind, while Lasso continued to act as a smokescreen before Dihya's eyes. Every word, every gesture was calculated to sow chaos.

Tarakna's plan was working perfectly. But at what cost? As he savored his triumph, a part of him couldn't help wondering whether, by crossing that line, he hadn't awakened forces he could no longer control. The moral dilemma turned into a silent torment, leaving Tarakna to face an unavoidable truth: sometimes, even the most brilliant minds can be consumed by their own creations.

Tarakna wanted to drive Kenneth mad enough to have him committed to a psychiatric hospital, but in the end, remorse consumed him from within, just like his victim. As he sat on a bus on his way home, he rethought his whole plan, his real motives and the result he had achieved. Kenneth's suffering was evident in the communications, and this made him very uncomfortable. Not wanting to prolong the torment any further, he decided to disconnect the clones as soon as he returned home.

As he stepped off the bus, his watch began to vibrate. It was Dihya receiving a phone call. Tarakna transferred the call to his headset and listened in.

- Hello, Dihya, it's Mr. Hanfman.

- Hello master.

- What I'm about to tell you isn't easy. You'll have to be strong.

- What's going on? Please tell me...

Dihya's heart began to beat frantically and her hands trembled like leaves. She couldn't finish her sentence.

- Unfortunately, Kenneth took his own life in prison, Mr. Hanfman let out of his mouth in an almost dead voice. Be strong, Dihya. He's left you a letter, which I'll give you when you want it.

Dihya screamed with all her might, dropping her phone. Her legs no longer held her. She collapsed to the floor, sprawled like a lifeless corpse, her eyes turned towards the ceiling. The scream pierced Tarakna's soul, and he froze, unable to look away from the tragedy he had orchestrated. Every inch of him was torn between bitter victory and crushing guilt.

Chapter 67

Tarakna was shocked. He clearly didn't want to achieve this result. Back at home, all he could do was sit in oppressive silence and contemplate the extent of his destructive work. Guilt gnawed at him, but he knew he had to act, if only to mitigate the consequences of his actions.

After spending a while pondering what to do next, he gradually came to his senses and decided to find a way forward. He chose to leave Kenneth's clone alive, thinking it might bring some semblance of comfort to Dihya. She could continue to chat with the clone if she wished, finding some of her devastated love. With Lasso no longer any reason to exist, Tarakna gave the clone back its original name, Asklepios, "he who revives the dead".

Tarakna programmed Asklepios to automatically pick up Dihya's calls, every other time on average. This way, the clone wouldn't be triggered all the time, maintaining a certain distance and reminding Dihya that Kenneth was indeed dead and that she was talking to a machine. It was his way of preventing her from falling into the dreaded Eliza effect.

***

The Eliza effect is a psychological phenomenon where people attribute feelings and human intelligence to a computer program, particularly when interacting with a chatbot or natural language processing system. The term comes from a computer program called ELIZA, developed in the 1960s by Joseph Weizenbaum. ELIZA simulated a conversation with a psychotherapist by rephrasing users' answers in the form of questions, thus creating the illusion of real understanding.

The phenomenon is often used to illustrate how people can anthropomorphize machines, i.e. attribute human characteristics to them, even when the program operates with very simple algorithms and no real understanding of human language or emotions. The Eliza effect shows how human interactions can be influenced by responses perceived as empathetic or intelligent, even when generated by machines.

***

In this way, Tarakna hoped to prevent Dihya from entering into an improbable situation where she might become really attached to the clone and end up believing that Kenneth was alive. This reminder, though painful, would be useful for her. Tarakna didn't want to sow any more evil after the drama he'd caused.

Chapter 68

Dihya, stunned by the shock of her fall to the ground, slowly came to her senses. The sky literally seemed to be falling after the suicide of her lover, Kenneth. Pain pierced every fiber of her being, a heavy weight settling in her chest, almost preventing her from breathing. Yet she knew she had to understand what had happened.

With hesitant but determined steps, she made her way to the home of lawyer Mr. Hanfman. The streets of Paris whizzed by, each bend adding to her confusion. At one point, she narrowly missed running over a motorcyclist. The shrill sound of the horn momentarily brought her back to reality, but despair plunged her into a dangerous unconsciousness. She accelerated, determined to find answers.

When she arrived at the law firm, she rushed to see Mr. Hanfman. The lawyer, a stern-looking man with a compassionate gaze, gave her a long hug. She felt a wave of comfort flow through her, but it wasn't enough to ease her pain.

- Dihya, I'm so sorry about what happened, he murmured.

Although he knew the details of the tragedy in Kenneth's cell, he hesitated to share them with her, for fear of deepening her grief. Finally, he settled for handing her a letter, his hands trembling.

- Kenneth left me this for you, he said, his eyes betraying a deep sadness.

Dihya took the letter, her heart racing. The lawyer's words seemed to echo in her mind as she left the office, the letter clutched to her chest. Back at home, she sat down at the kitchen table, unable to wait any longer. Her hands trembled as she tore open the envelope.

Kenneth's first words seemed written with a desperate intensity, each sentence a painful farewell. Dihya's tears were already flowing as she began to read.

She paused, unable to continue, the words blurring through her tears. Each sentence was a dagger in her heart, bringing her closer to the abyss into which Kenneth had sunk. Yet she knew she had to read to the end, for him, for them.

= =

My dear Dihya,

As you read this letter, I know that you feel immense pain and deep incomprehension. Above all, I want you to know that I would never have wanted you to suffer like this. My heart breaks at the thought of leaving you in such distress, but I see no other way out.

I proclaim my innocence, Dihya. I never committed the acts for which I have been unjustly accused. From day one, I've been the victim of a machination that I still don't fully understand. I tried to fight, to resist this injustice, but the weight of these accusations finally got the better of me.

I'm exhausted, Dihya. Exhausted by this never-ending struggle, by the anguish and despair that overtake me more and more every day. Prison isn't just a physical cage, it's a mental torture that's slowly consuming me. Every day, I sink deeper into the darkness, and I can no longer see the light at the end of this tunnel.

I want you to know that my love for you has never wavered. You've been my strength, my support, and my reason for carrying on in spite of everything. But now I'm at the end of my rope. I can't go on living like this, watching you suffer for me, carrying this burden that's destroying us both.

I beg your forgiveness for what I'm about to do. It's not a decision I took lightly, but I believe it's the only way for me to finally find peace. My mind is exhausted, and my body can't keep up. I don't want to be a burden to you anymore, or see you eaten away by this sadness.

Remember our moments of happiness, our love, and all that we shared. Don't let this tragedy erase the happy memories we created together on the beautiful island of Crete. Live your life to the full, be happy, and find within yourself the strength to carry on. You are a wonderful person, and you deserve all the joy in the world.

Farewell, Dihya. I'll always love you, even beyond this life. Forgive me for leaving you like this, but believe me, it's the only way I can see to ease my suffering.

With all my love,

===============================

Dihya stared at the letter for a long moment, Kenneth's words seeming to float before her tear-fogged eyes. She slowly brought it to her chest and clasped it with both hands, desperately seeking to capture a last vestige of his presence, a final connection through the paper. It was as if she could almost smell his scent, hear his laughter, feel the warmth of his arms around her.

An immense sadness overcame her, an overwhelming wave of pain and grief that completely overwhelmed her. Tears continued to flow from her large, reddened eyes, each drop symbolizing a fragment of her broken heart. Memories of Kenneth, of their moments of shared happiness, flashed through her mind, intensifying her suffering still further.

Chapter 69

Dihya stood in a state of total confusion. Kenneth, though imprisoned and suffering, had shown no sign of the impending tragedy. The mystery, which had thickened daily since his return from the island of Crete, now seemed almost unfathomable.

Kenneth, from the letter he left her, seemed innocent. This affair held many secrets that Dihya was determined to uncover. Her sadness and nostalgia led her to spend hours reviewing her last Skype conversations with Kenneth, desperately looking for the slightest clue as to what was going to happen. There was no sign of suicide. Yet, with each viewing, there was one scene that always intrigued her: the one in which Kenneth explained the absence of the tattoo on his arm. This anomaly, which was obvious to Dihya, seemed strange to her. Kenneth's explanation seemed light, even if she wasn't an expert in technology or videos.

Various scenarios ran through Dihya's mind. To cut short her overactive imagination, she decided to consult a friend in a good position to give her a serious explanation. She picked up the phone and asked to be put through.

- Siri, call Sulas.

The phone lit up, displaying her friend's name, and placed the call. A few seconds later, a familiar voice answered.

- Hello, Dihya, how are you?

- Hi, Sulas, it's okay, thank you.

- So, you're looking for something to write about? I warn you, I've got nothing at the moment. My current experiments aren't finished yet. You'll have to wait a few days.

- No, I'm calling about something else.

- OK, get to the point then. I don't have much time.

- Listen, I have a video on my phone that intrigues me and I don't know what to make of it. Can I come over and show it to you?

- Can't you just send it to me?

- No, it's on Skype and I'm not sure how to get it out.

Sulas was going to tell her how to do it, but he soon realized that it would probably take longer than getting her to come.

- Go ahead, bring it and we'll take a look.

Dihya hung up without even saying goodbye and set off for Sulas' company, her mind still in turmoil.

On the way, memories of Crete flooded into Dihya's mind. She remembered the walks on the sunny beach, the endless discussions on the terrace of Casa Delfino under the starry sky, and the hope she and Kenneth shared for the future. How had all this turned into a nightmare? Why had Kenneth been arrested? Was he really as innocent as he claimed? Why had he committed suicide? So many questions that remained unanswered, but perhaps not for long, thanks to her friend. He was her only hope.

Chapter 70

Sulas stood in front of his screens, watching numbers and codes fly by at dizzying speed. This expert in artificial intelligence had managed to capture the world's attention a few months earlier by dramatically redefining the Turing test. He had created an AI, a digital clone fed with his own personal data, and given it control over his social networking accounts. The aim was simple, but audacious: to see how long it would take Internet users to discover that they were conversing with a machine.

Sulas monitored every interaction, every comment. But after a month, despite intense and passionate exchanges on his widely-followed accounts, no one had uncovered the deception. Sulas' satisfaction was palpable when he published a long article on his blog, detailing the results of his experiment. He announced the publication on all his social networks, with a link to his blog. Dihya, convinced of the importance of the subject, wrote an excellent article for the Herald, but media attention was quickly diverted to more sensational global crises.

Sulas, however, had not said his last word. Despite his public announcement ending the experiment and disconnecting the AI from his networks, he had actually started the second phase of his project. This time, he wanted to see if, now that people had been warned of his dirty tricks, they would be more vigilant. He restarted his AI, letting it interact freely again.

A month later, the result was the same: Internet users, though more alert, fell for the scam once again. Sulas published his results, this time with irrefutable proof. A video showed his screen where posts and comments were automatically published by the AI, followed by his appearance in the camera frame to demonstrate any lack of direct intervention on his part. This time, the reaction was immediate and explosive. The world's media seized on the story, talking about it non-stop for weeks.

The impact of this revelation was profound and long-lasting. Internet users became wary, doubt creeping into every online interaction. Exchanges on social networks took a different, more cautious turn. Humorous and ironic comments proliferated: "Who am I talking to again?", "Hi machine, you're looking hot, are you sure your fan's running properly?", "There you go, he's activated his twin again". The term "*twin*" quickly became popular to designate an AI that manages social accounts for users. Within weeks, many digital platforms, including Sulas, were offering this service, transforming the dynamics of social networking forever.

But the story didn't end there. Sulas, a true pioneer, saw even further ahead. He knew that AI and humans were at the dawn of a new era of collaboration and cohabitation. The results of his new experiments were eagerly awaited, but would have to wait for some time yet.

Chapter 71

Dihya hurried towards the offices of Sulas' company, not far from her home. Night had fallen and the premises were almost deserted, with only a few employees still at their posts. After the usual greetings, Dihya took out her phone and searched for the video they were to talk about, before handing it to Sulas.

- There, that's the video. Take a good look at the guy's arm, she said insistently.

- He's quite muscular, your guy. Who is he? asked Sulas, laughing.

- His name is Kenneth. He's a friend I met recently.

Sulas, without trying to find out more about Dihya's private life, concentrated on the video, his gaze staring intently at the screen. After viewing the recording, he broke the silence.

- Let's be clear. A spontaneous disruption in the video stream, removing just one tattoo, is almost impossible. We're more likely to be hit by an asteroid tomorrow. To me, there are only two possibilities: either someone intercepted the video stream and deliberately deleted the tattoo, which implies phone hacking, or the man in the video is not Kenneth. A twin, perhaps? I'm leaning towards the second option, as I can't see why anyone would bother deleting a simple tattoo.

- No, that's not possible, Dihya retorted firmly. In other videos, it's different.

She picked up her phone again, frantically searching for another recording showing the tattoo, but found nothing. She hadn't saved the conversation where Kenneth had shown her his tattooed arm after her curious request.

- I promise you that in other conversations, I could see the tattoo, insisted Dihya.

Sulas looked at her, an almost mocking smile on his lips.

- I swear, added Dihya, I did see the tattoo during some Skype conversations. At least once, I'd asked him and he'd shown it to me. It's a letter, kappa to be exact.

Suddenly, she remembered she had a photo of the symbol. Searching through her text messages with Kenneth, she found it.

- Look, that's it, she said, showing Sulas the photo.

He glanced at Dihya's phone before smiling broadly.

- That's what I'm talking about, a twin.

Dihya didn't understand what Sulas was getting at, but knew he never spoke lightly. His arguments were often solid and borne out.

- When I say twin, I'm not necessarily talking about a physical twin. It could be a digital twin. These days, it's not impossible. Remember the twins, my experience that you yourself reported in the Herald? Are you sure you haven't talked to a twin?

Dihya began to consider this possibility, although not yet entirely convinced.

- Yes, but I wasn't communicating with Kenneth in writing, she argued. I was talking to him via Skype and seeing him live.

- It's true that images make things technically more complicated, but not impossible. Haven't you heard of deepfakes?

- Do you think I'm stupid? retorted Dihya, annoyed. Of course, I know about deepfakes, but why would the tattoo be visible on some communications and not others? I don't agree with you.

- If it were a deepfake, it would only activate if the creator decided to, right? retorted Sulas. He'd be the one controlling it. Like twins on social networks, it's up to the user. I don't know why it was intermittent in your Skype calls with Kenneth, but I think it's the only plausible explanation.

Dihya knew about deepfakes, having written about them before, but she didn't think the technology was advanced enough to integrate them into live video. Yet Sulas' explanation finally convinced her.

This new perspective opened up an abyss of dizzying deepfakes-related possibilities. She remained silent, trying to piece together the whole story in her mind.

Chapter 72

Dihya was deeply disgusted. The idea that she'd been duped into talking to a machine, mistaking it for Kenneth, enraged her.

- But why do we let people play with fire and develop such horrors? It's obvious that madmen were going to get hold of it to do harm.

Sulas, not quite agreeing, tried to explain with benevolent patience.

- The person who implemented this deepfake was certainly an expert and above all a highly motivated person, and believe me, he's way ahead of what's out there right now. So, he didn't use an off-the-shelf tool. Seeing the Skype videos, and without the tattoo story, I personally would never have guessed it was a fake.

Sulas' words echoed in Dihya's head. If an expert like him couldn't detect anything, then what about the average person? A question was burning in her mind that might well put her on the trail of the truth in Kenneth's case.

- You're telling me that you wouldn't have been able to guess the deepfake without my information. Would it be the same for a policeman who didn't know the whole story?

- Absolutely, replied Sulas with quiet certainty. No policeman, no matter how qualified, could detect it. Still, this is my field, and I know what's doable and what isn't. At this level of perfection, it's just not possible. At this level of perfection, it's just impossible.

- Even if you have access to the video? I mean the file, clarified Dihya, her piercing gaze scanning her friend's face.

Sulas then tried an analogy to clarify his point.

- You know, it's like doping or counterfeiting money. Before a tool can detect a counterfeit currency obtained with a brand new technique, the currency must first be analyzed for specific flaws. Only then is the detection tool perfected. Counterfeiters and cheats in sport are always one step ahead. We sometimes try to anticipate, but it's not easy. It also takes a lot of resources.

Dihya nodded, absorbing every word.

- I understand perfectly. Thank you for your time.

Still unsure of the possibilities and limits of these deepfake technologies, Dihya wanted one last clarification from her friend.

- Say Sulas, could we do the same thing with a CCTV camera? I mean, insert a deepfake into a recording without it showing?

Sulas took a moment before answering.

- Yes, it makes no difference. Of course, you'd have to be able to access the video stream, by hacking into the camera management server if you're not authorized to do so. Technically, it's possible.

Sulas's answer was all Dihya needed to believe a little more in Kenneth's innocence. Silently, she told herself that the CCTV images of Kenneth's office had surely been altered by a deepfake that the police had no choice but to use as irrefutable proof of guilt. The problem was, it was impossible for anyone to prove otherwise today!

Chapter 73

Dihya was paralyzed at the thought of these sophisticated deepfakes. It called so many things into question, starting with her profession as a journalist. For the justice system, which had perhaps just sentenced an innocent man to death on false evidence, it was already done!

- Do you realize that the arrival of these undetectable deepfakes will upset the very foundations of society? It's a horror, this thing.

Sulas, aware of his friend's torment, tried to comfort her. He tried to lighten the mood by initiating a diversion, a mischievous smile on his lips.

- For once, you've given me the opportunity to challenge you on your own turf, history. You talk about the arrival of deepfakes. Do you know when the first one was created?

Dihya smiled, implicitly admitting her ignorance.

- I'm not sure, around 2018 with the Obama deepfake?

- No, I'm talking about the story you love, the real one, the old one.

- Now you've got me stumped. I have no idea.

- We'll proceed in stages, suggested Sulas. Who invented the incandescent light bulb?

Dihya burst out laughing, not seeing the connection with today's topic.

- I don't know what you're getting at, but I remember very well what I learned at school. It's Thomas Edison, of course!

Sulas laughed in turn, and Dihya understood that something was wrong with his answer.

- You see, this alone could be called a fake, or even a deepfake, such is the depth and antiquity of this false belief. In fact, it was the British scientist Joseph Swan who demonstrated in 1860 that the incandescence of a carbon filament could be prolonged in a vacuum. He patented the process. It wasn't until 1879, almost twenty years later, when vacuum pumps were perfected, that Swan and Edison presented a functional light bulb. A lawsuit ensued, and Joseph Swan was given credit. But that wasn't all.

- I can hear it, but I still don't see the link with deepfakes, Dihya interrupted.

- Edison was a real trickster. Several months before his 1879 presentation, he informed journalists that they would each receive a private demonstration of his new light bulb. They could admire his work at his Menlo Park laboratory, but he made sure to get them out quickly before the bulb burned out. That was the main problem at the time. Many others had failed before him and Swan. The bulb lasted only a few seconds because of the bamboo filament used by Edison. His plan worked, and the gullible press raved about a "perfect" invention. This fake news caused a mini financial crisis in London, with gas prices plummeting. In reality, it was only by adopting Swan's patented carbon filament that Edison was able to demonstrate the durability of his bulb and industrialize it.

- The Americans have always been good at this kind of manipulation, added Dihya. I'm not surprised.

- But I'm not done yet, Sulas interrupted. Now comes the real deepfake story. The light bulb story was just an introduction. Edison had built an empire, touching many fields.

In 1898, projected cinema had only been in use in the United States for two years when the Spanish-American War broke out. Cuba was seeking to free itself from Spanish domination, and tensions were at their highest. The sinking of the USS Maine in Havana triggered a media avalanche, prompting the United States to declare war on Spain. Pro-war propaganda used a film entitled "*Shooting Captured Insurgents*".

As the political crisis in Cuba deepened, the Edison film company saw an opportunity. Under the name Edison War-Graph, it contributed to the propaganda effort. Its cameraman embarked with the American troops and shot images of the wreck of the Maine and the raising of the American flag, but returned to Florida before the fighting began. The rest of the film was shot in New Jersey, in the United States. It showed Cuban insurgents being shot by Spanish soldiers. The most sensitive part of Edison's propaganda video was therefore purely and simply a fake.

Dihya nodded, her friend was right.

- I'm still thinking about that story about the light bulb and Edison, confided Dihya. It's been taught in every school since I can remember. It's just crazy!

- Yes, Americans are very good at imposing certain beliefs. They've professionalized public relations, remember Edward Bernays.

Dihya, worried and not wanting to dwell on another subject that could take hours, returned to deepfakes.

- If the rudimentary means of the 19ᵉ century were able to deceive people to such an extent, what can we say now with this AI filth?

Sulas sensed the dismay in Dihya's voice, but tried to nuance it.

- Yes, but don't condemn everything. AI is useful for many applications. Deepfakes can also be used positively in certain fields.

- What? Useful deepfakes applications? Stop it, or I'll get angry. Can't you see that this will be a massacre for society? No one will know right from wrong. There's no way to check.

Sulas stood up and walked over to a touch screen projected onto a pane of glass near his desk, ready to show Dihya something.

Chapter 74

Sulas murmured something to his connected watch, triggering the launch of a YouTube video clip on the screen projected onto the glass. Two actors were deep in conversation.

- Do you recognize this? asked Sulas, his eyes shining with curiosity.

- Yes, it's the film "Top Gun: Maverick" with Tom Cruise. I saw it when it came out, replied Dihya, a nostalgic smile on her lips. Here, in this scene, we see Iceman, played by Val Kilmer.

- Exactly! I see you're still a fan of action films. I just want you to know that without the deepfake, this scene wouldn't have been possible.

- And why is that? asked Dihya, intrigued.

- Simply because, at the time of filming, Val Kilmer was suffering from throat cancer. He could no longer speak. Thanks to AI, his voice was recreated. For the cinema, deepfakes are an unhoped-for invention. Imagine: all dead actors could reappear on screen. Wouldn't a new chapter in The Godfather with Marlon Brando as Don Vito Corleone be great? Especially with today's means.

- Yes, I admit I wouldn't say no to a Marilyn Monroe comeback, confided Dihya, dreamily.

- There's also advertising, continued Sulas, before whispering to his watch. A new clip started up.

- Is that Bruce Lee? exclaimed a surprised Dihya.

- Of course it's him. It's a 2013 ad for Johnnie Walker, created with a deepfake. Well, I admit the result wasn't great and the ad pretty lame. Using a sportsman like Bruce Lee to sell Whisky wasn't great. But deepfake technology has come a long way since then, as you'll see. Check out this other, much more successful ad.

Sulas brought another video clip to the screen. This time, it was an advertisement from 2023 starring Catherine Deneuve for the luxury house Cartier. The clip showed her in four scenes reminiscent of films from her career, at different times. The result was breathtaking.

- Ah yes, that's really well done, acknowledged Dihya, impressed.

- You can see right away why deepfakes are so interesting for the cinema. Making an actor look younger or older is now child's play. No need for masks and make-up. And with AI, translations are on another level. Actors' lips and voices now adapt to different languages. Isn't it incredible that all the actors are multilingual? A translation that used to cost a fortune and take an inordinate amount of time is now possible in a matter of hours. Oh, and don't forget video games. With deepfake, any player can make a character look like themselves or someone else, simply by providing a photo.

Dihya interrupted Sulas, still skeptical.

- I see, but all you're saying is entertainment.

- True, but think about education too. A picture is worth a thousand words, isn't it? Students retain better what they see. Imagine a video of Rosa Parks explaining segregation, Eisenhower talking about World War II, or Einstein describing relativity. Just imagine!

- Do you think you're Martin Luther King with your "imagine" or what? Calm down, retorted Dihya, laughing.

Sulas smiled before continuing.

- I've saved the best for last regarding deepfakes.

- Go ahead, make me dream, said Dihya, her voice heavy with irony.

- Well, in the media and information!

- Ah, that I did see. My newspaper's been decimated by the AI, said Dihya in disappointment.

- No, I'm talking about deepfakes, retorted Sulas. In China, for example, TV news and home shopping presenters are pure deepfakes.

- Obviously, China. All the dirty stuff starts there.

- No, think again. Look at the Ukraine. They're our friends, aren't they? Let me show you something.

Sulas made another request to his watch and a video began to play. A young woman appeared on the screen, her voice deep and confident:

"Dear members of the media and the public, welcome. My name is Victoria Shi. I was created by the Ukrainian Ministry of Foreign Affairs using artificial intelligence to provide you with timely and quality information on consular affairs.

I'm a digital person. This means that the text you hear has not been read by a real person. It was generated by artificial intelligence.

I will perform a number of tasks. First, I will inform the public by providing verified and timely information from Ukrainian consular services. I will provide journalists with updates on the work of consuls in protecting the rights and interests of Ukrainian citizens abroad. I will also inform you about the Foreign Ministry's response to incidents and emergencies abroad.

In the bottom corner of this video, you can see a QR code. It leads to the official website of the Ministry of Foreign Affairs... "

Sulas interrupted the sequence.

- You see, this video is a deepfake. This character was created from scratch by the AI to save time and resources in times of war, he explained. At least, that was the argument put forward by the Ukrainian authorities at the time.

- An effective way of getting rid of the cameramen and all the technicians, retorted Dihya, increasingly disillusioned.

- No, there's more to it than that. Writing propaganda speeches takes time and communication experts. In the midst of war, you need to react quickly, and AI can accomplish this in the blink of an eye. What's more, with its powers of persuasion, a human can't compete with an AI like ChatGPT. In my opinion, that's another reason.

- I don't doubt it. Even my cautious self was fooled into thinking I was talking to a human for days.

- Well, let me show you one last thing, suggested Sulas, before turning to his watch: "Go to the ARTE channel replay and put on the documentary 'We, the youth of Iran'. Play the video from the 5th minute mark."

A fraction of a second later, the documentary launched onto the screen. Right from the start, Iranian women were testifying to the restrictions on their freedom under the Islamic regime. Sulas paused the video before calling out to Dihya.

- What do these images inspire in you?

- What do you want me to say? These women are brave, but I fear for their lives.

- That's just it, they're safe.

- This is the land of the mullahs, I remind you. They'll put them in jail, at best.

Sulas burst out laughing.

- These girls are deepfakes. They have been generated by AI.

Sulas paused the film before starting the replay again, this time from the beginning. A warning then appeared in the preamble:

> To preserve the safety of the witnesses in this film, names and locations have been changed.
>
> Some faces have been anonymized using artificial intelligence.

Every time a sequence shows a deepfake, a banner appears at the bottom of the screen: "Faces modified with artificial intelligence".

Seeing this, Dihya exploded with anger.

- I'm appalled. We've opened Pandora's box by using these deepfakes in our business. I understand that it strengthens the narrative by showing uncovered faces, as opposed to anonymous testimonies which always sow a little doubt in the viewer's mind. But it's going to create uncertainty about everything else. What if journalists don't always warn and use fakes for pure propaganda, to blindly support the policy in place? Our credibility is already being damaged, and fewer and fewer people are taking us seriously. The slightest misstep and everything will collapse. No one will believe anything!

Sulas let Dihya digest all the information she had just heard before bringing her back to the purpose of her presence in his offices.

- Let's get back to our main topic, Dihya. What do you intend to do about this Kenneth business?

Chapter 75

Dihya dropped onto a rolling office chair and, with a vigorous push of her feet, slid towards Sulas, her face hardened with determination.

- I want to know the truth, the whole truth about this dark affair, declared Dihya with unshakeable resolve.

- I can imagine, but it won't be easy. Whoever's behind all this must be pretty sly, Sulas replied thoughtfully.

- The question is: are you ready to help me or not?

- Of course I'll help you, you're my friend. But how? We don't have access to the cabinet's recording, it's with the police. So, on that front, there's nothing to hope for. That leaves your Skype conversations.

- Yes, can't we exploit that?

- As I explained to you, the deepfake is almost perfect, except for the tattoo, but that's a detail that wouldn't do us any good. Let me think about it.

Dihya moved away and headed for the balcony's glass door to take a look at the streets of Paris, leaving Sulas deep in thought. Just as she was about to open the door to go out for a breath of fresh air, Sulas leapt from his armchair, as if illuminated by a revelation.

- I may have an idea. Do you have access to Kenneth's Skype account?

- No, I don't have access, but we could try. I've got his phone number and we'll try something for the password.

- Look, if whoever's behind this hasn't deactivated the clone, we could try to trigger it by making a Skype call.

- I'm not sure what you want to do.

- We'll proceed in stages. First, let's try to get into Kenneth's Skype account. Give me his number.

Dihya took out her phone to check Kenneth's number before dictating it to Sulas.

- All right, then. What do you suggest for a password, since you obviously know him so well?

Dihya thought for a long moment before breaking the silence.

- I think I've got an idea. When I was talking to him, he told me that the police couldn't open his PC even though he'd given them the right password. When I told him he might have made a mistake, he said he had the same all-purpose password and that's how he opened all his accounts, even when he was in prison.

- And do you have any idea what his code is?

- Yes, he gave it to me to access his bank account, because the application is not allowed in prison. He wanted me to transfer money to his lawyer.

- Go ahead then, hand it over.

Dihya grabs a pen and writes a series of signs on a post-it note:

Magali@1996

Sulas entered the sequence before validating. Access was denied.

- No, it doesn't work, Dihya. Are you sure about that?

- Yes, I'm quite sure. This is what I used for the bank. It's his ex-wife's name and her year of birth. Please try again.

- OK, I'll try again.

Sulas grasped the signs once more before validating. It was another refusal.

- Careful, the account may be permanently blocked if you make another mistake, warns Sulas. But there's one thing I don't understand. Did he keep his ex-girlfriend's name when he was supposed to be in love with you? If I were him, I'd have changed it.

- Oh dear, you remind me of something. When he gave me the password, he was a bit embarrassed and told me he'd already changed it on his other accounts, except for the bank, since he didn't have access to it.

- You see? That's not it after all. But wait, let's do a bit of psychology here. Lazy as he is, the man rarely changes his habits. What if we applied his logic to the new password he'd chosen? Knowing that you're his new girlfriend, we could have something like your name and date of birth. Couldn't we?

- If you like, we could try "Dihya@1998".

Sulas typed in the new character string, then validated. Disappointment appeared on his face.

- No, that's not it, unfortunately.

Dihya thought for a long moment before snatching the phone from Sulas' hands.

- Here, I'll try another trick.

Dihya slowly entered letter after letter of a new password:

Kahina@1998

She pressed "Validate", her heart racing. A fraction of a second later, a broad smile appeared on her face.

- Yes, I did it. The account is open.

Sulas, having seen what Dihya had grasped, understood that it was her nickname that had to be introduced. He himself often called her that, but hadn't thought of it.

- Great! Now that we have access to the account, we can move on to the next step. I'm going to ask you to open your Skype and call Kenneth.

- Are you crazy? Kenneth is dead, I remind you, he won't answer.

- Yes, Kenneth is dead, I know that, but maybe his clone isn't if his creator hasn't deactivated him as I explained to you earlier. We'd pretend Kenneth was still alive and you'd give him a call.

Dihya, doubtful, picked up her phone and tried to reach Kenneth on Skype as usual. After two rings, Sulas picked up the call on his end before asking Dihya a few questions.

What do you see on your camera?

- Well, your head! You're the one who picks up the phone, who else do you want me to see?

- OK, cut and we'll do it again, said Sulas, impatiently.

Dihya hung up and tried a second time. When Sulas picked up for the second time, the result was still the same.

- You see? Your bullshit theory doesn't make any sense, irritated Dihya. What other X-Files scenario would you suggest to me now?

Aware of everything she'd been through, Sulas didn't hold it against her. He tried to explain again.

- But I thought I'd made myself clear about the deepfake. If the tattoo was only visible on certain conversations, the activation of the clone was necessarily intermittent. That's what we're seeing here. The clone doesn't activate. Maybe the third attempt will be the right one. Shall we try again?

Dihya, resigned, didn't believe in the chances of the plan proposed by her friend. She remained inert. Sulas grabbed her phone before it locked and tried his luck alone. He initiated the call on Dihya's phone before picking up his own a second later. Without warning, a sound emerged from Dihya's phone. It was Kenneth's voice.

- Hi honey, how are you?

Sulas, panic-stricken, tossed the phone into Dihya's hands before slipping away to a nearby office.

- Hi, there.

This brief word of greeting was the only one to escape from Dihya's tetanized mouth.

With the last Sulas employees having deserted the company some time ago, a deathly silence pervaded the premises. Only the siren of an ambulance racing through Paris could be heard in the distance.

Chapter 76

Dihya preferred to put an end to the discussion and hung up the phone. She called Sulas, urging him to leave his hiding place and come over for a chat.

- Sorry, murmured Dihya, her voice trembling. I couldn't continue the conversation with the deepfake. It was too hard for me.

Sulas looked at her with compassion visible in his eyes.

- Don't worry, he said gently. I understand you. It's not an easy situation.

A solitary tear rolled down Dihya's cheek before she quickly wiped it away.

- I mustn't give up now, she asserted with renewed determination. Now that we know it was a deepfake that infiltrated the Skype conversations, it's obvious that someone had it in for Kenneth. I'm sure it's the same for the cabinet recording. But there's nothing to prove it yet.

Sulas nodded, thinking hard.

- The only way to prove Kenneth's innocence is to find the deepfake designer and make him confess. I don't see any other way.

- Yes, probably. But Kenneth must have known he had an enemy. Yet he never told me, even though he confided so much about his private life.

- Maybe it's not too late, replied Sulas with an enigmatic smile. We know his clone is still active, don't we?

- Yes, but so what?

- Isn't a clone, by definition, supposed to behave exactly like the original?

- Do you really think the clone could reveal things to us the way Kenneth would? I find that hard to believe.

- Whoever created the clone certainly had access to all Kenneth's personal data. In other words, the clone integrated this information during its training. If Kenneth had an enemy, there must be traces in this data, and therefore in the clone. By asking him the right questions, we could get some answers.

Dihya was speechless. It was both logical and terrifying.

- The problem is that time is against us, warned Sulas. The designer could deactivate the clone at any time, and we'd lose everything forever. Now that Kenneth is dead, he has no interest in keeping the clone active. We have to act fast. You're a journalist, you know how to ask the right questions.

What Sulas didn't know was that Tarakna had left the clone active out of pity for Dihya. A priori, they had all the time they needed. But if Tarakna discovered their plan, he could rush in and pull the plug.

Dihya, trying to follow the reasoning, proposed an idea.

- You're right about that. But what's stopping us from creating our own Kenneth clone? You're the best AI expert I know.

- I wish I could, but I don't have the material.

- What material?

- Don't pretend, Dihya. I'm obviously talking about Kenneth's personal data.

- So how did the designer do it?

- He probably hacked into Kenneth's phone and other devices.

- Of course. I'm so confused, I lose track.

Dihya regained her composure before returning to the solution proposed by Sulas.

- If I've understood your proposal correctly, I need to talk to the clone for as long as possible and ask him the right questions to get as much information as possible. I'm going to make myself some coffee.

- You're right, you're right. You've got some rough nights ahead. Unless we can find a faster way.

- What way? asked Dihya, intrigued.

- What do you do when you need to fill a bottle from a tap quickly?

- I turn the tap on full blast, of course.

- Exactly the same. It's the same with the clone. You have to open its mouth wide so that it spits out as much information as possible.

Chapter 77

Dihya's brain was boiling under the pressure. Although she had grasped all of Sulas's explanations, a mental fatigue was beginning to invade her. She could feel her reasoning abilities weakening.

- But what about a machine? asked Dihya, her tiredness showing in her voice.

- Imagine increasing the flow of water by turning on the tap, explained Sulas. Here, we're increasing the amount of data by making the clone work harder. Let's take a calculator. If it takes you ten seconds to enter a multiplication and the result is instantaneous, you can perform six operations per minute. Write faster, say in five seconds, and you double the operations per minute, i.e. twelve. That's easy, isn't it?

- Ah, I see. I need to talk faster and ask the clone as many questions as possible.

- Exactly.

- I have to be a war machine to keep up. You overestimate my abilities, my friend. Well, I'll get to it.

- Wait, wait, I haven't finished.

- What now? retorted Dihya, startled.

- War machine, that's what I like to hear. Let's go back to the beginning. The designer built a clone with whom you were unknowingly chatting. Meanwhile, Kenneth was also talking to someone. Who do you think?

- With a clone of me. Makes sense. Kenneth couldn't believe it either.

- Exactly. To hold everything together, we had to maintain the illusion of real two-way communication.

- It makes sense, but I hadn't thought of it.

- To make Kenneth's clone talk and get as much information as possible, we'll have to recreate your clone. It'll be faster than you and won't get tired. My deepfake project has just delivered excellent results. We'll exploit that. Your clone will be our war machine! Got it?

- You're an ace, Sulas. You're an ace!

- Also, we'll be using the written word more often for discussions. We'll go much faster, and Kenneth's clone will turn into a chatbot, responding just as quickly.

- You're a genius, I love you.

- Wait, I haven't told you everything yet, added Sulas proudly.

- It's not over yet?

- I've saved the best for last.

Sulas opened a can of soda and took a few sips to refresh himself. After a busy day, he too was showing signs of fatigue. His dry throat made conversation difficult.

After relieving his thirst, Sulas continued:

- You, Dihya, are a journalist, good at asking the right questions. That's an asset.

- Thank you, a compliment at last!

- Not so fast. I said you were good, not the best. Your clone will also be a good journalist, but we'll accompany him with a communications expert. A specialized AI will guide your clone to ask the best questions and reveal the truth. This guide, our Oracle, will communicate with your clone. If necessary, we'll use ChatGPT, a generalist but effective tool.

- That's just great. In my business, we call that blowing into an earpiece!

- Exactly. But here, several AIs communicate, not humans.

- Okay, no time to lose. What do I have to do?

- I need access to all your devices and social network accounts.

- What? All my privacy?

- Sorry, but we have no choice. To build your clone, I need as much of your personal data as possible. In any case, the designer already has them and could divulge them at any time if he wished. So, you'd better find him before he does something irreparable.

- You're right, there's no time to lose. Let's make it quick.

Chapter 78

Sulas, anticipating the next move with disconcerting precision, called a friend, Cylia, to the rescue. A renowned influencer, followed by millions on Instagram and TikTok, Cylia shares every moment of her life online, from breakfasts to movies watched at night. Nothing escapes her fans. When Sulas proposed a clone project using a deepfake a few months ago, she jumped at the chance with enthusiasm. She was already familiar with the phenomenon of virtual influencers such as Aitana Lopez or Lil Miquela, with millions of followers and attracting the attention of luxury and automotive brands. For Cylia, eager to get rich, the Sulas opportunity was a godsend: travel while her clone entertains her fans.

Sulas made a Skype call to his friend Cylia. A few seconds later, she picked up.

- Hi Cylia.

- Hello Sulas.

Sulas, aware of the dangers of leaking personal data, was cautious in his communications. As he finalized his clone project, he knew that well-resourced enemies, such as the opposing intelligence services, could do better than him and get ahead of him. He had therefore devised a strategy to protect himself against the possibility of his communications being hacked. The Kenneth affair made this abundantly clear.

Immediately after taking Sulas' call, a ritual began between him and Cylia, leaving Dihya perplexed.

Cylia announced a color, "green", waited a moment, then Sulas replied "OK" before announcing another color, "yellow". Cylia nodded "OK".

Conversation naturally resumed.

- So, Sulas, what's going on?

- My dear Cylia, I have to help a friend, Dihya. We need your help.

- No worries. When is it due?

- Immediately. It's urgent.

- Tonight? Are you serious?

- Sorry, but you're our only chance.

- All right, then! But first a question. Where are you with my virtual clone?

- Almost finished. A few more adjustments. A matter of hours.

- All right! Here I come. You're gonna show me this.

- Thank you very much, Cylia. See you soon.

No sooner had Sulas hung up than Dihya rushed towards him, intrigued.

- What's all this about colors? Some weird cult?

Sulas burst out laughing.

- You should join our sect then, you would have avoided the traps of deepfakes on Skype.

- What do you mean by that? Explain quickly!

Sulas detailed the strange dialogue. The color announced by Cylia matched that of her left earring, and that announced by Sulas, the right earring he saw on the video transmitted via Skype. If the colors matched, confirmed with an OK, the chat was deemed safe. To further enhance security, Cylia regularly changed the colors of her earrings, LED gadgets controlled via an app.

In corporate videoconferencing, everyone had their own tricks for detecting deepfakes. In the past, a head turn was enough, but this technique was outdated. Today, it requires a prior identification protocol, applied to each connection with random variability, as with Cylia earrings.

Some cybersecurity companies had anticipated these hijackings and developed automated solutions, such as displays of random tokens to be presented in front of the camera. The code displayed was decrypted in real time and verified by the servers of the company providing the solution. If the code didn't match, communication was automatically cut off.

After detailing his trick and the more advanced solutions developed in the field of cybersecurity, Sulas stared Dihya in the eye.

- You see, I could have called Cylia directly, but I preferred to use Skype. I wanted to show you how simple it is to protect yourself in a world soon to be overrun by deepfakes.

- Really? Seriously, I'm never using that damn Skype again.

Sulas smiled.

- Ah, I doubt that very much.

Dihya frowned, reflecting on what she had just learned. She now understood the importance of caution in this new digital era, her eyes open to a disturbing reality, but one that was essential to grasp.

Chapter 79

Dihya had been isolated for hours in the small, dark office, lit only by the flickering glow of the monitor provided by Sulas. The oppressive silence was disturbed only by the persistent murmurs of her long discussions with Kenneth's clone. Unfortunately, no valuable information had emerged from these exchanges. Suddenly, Sulas' voice rang out, breaking the stillness of the moment.

- Come here, I've finished. Your clone is ready.

With her heart pounding, Dihya rushed to Sulas' office. As soon as she stepped through the door, a cold shiver ran down her spine. Before her, on the screen, stood her perfect double, a replica so exact it took her breath away.

- So, what do you think? Wait, I'll talk to her a little.

Sulas activated the clone and spoke a few words to her. Dihya froze and felt a strange sensation of vertigo. It was as if she had been torn from her own body, sucked into this digital reflection. The clone was so perfect that it was impossible to distinguish the original from the copy. Shock gripped her, and images from the Matrix movie flashed through her mind, including the scene where Morpheus asks Neo about the reality of dreams: "Have you ever had a dream, Neo, that seemed so real that if you'd never woken up, how could you tell the difference between the dream world and the real world?"

- It's downright terrifying. I imagine that, since you create and control it, you can make it say just about anything you want.

- Yes, of course. But for our purposes, I'm going to let the clone react and converse normally without any outside influence from me, apart from the directives he should receive from the oracle, the AI expert in communication.

- Wonderful! From now on, I'll be able to get all the crap out of my mouth and pin it on my clone, or vice versa, get my clone to say anything and everything and pin it on me. Welcome to the world of deepfakes!

Sulas smiled, a mischievous twinkle in his eye.

- Well, if you're still up for it, I'll start the conversation between your clone and Kenneth's and we'll see what happens. Go?

- Fingers crossed.

Sulas initiated the Skype call, and immediately afterwards, a deafening roar emanated from the computer bay, invading the company. The machines were running at full power, a sign that the exchanges between the clones were intense. Dihya anxiously watched the screen where her double and Kenneth's double were exchanging words, their voices mingling in a true-to-life digital symphony.

Time seemed to stand still. Each passing second increased the tension. The results would soon be in.

Chapter 80

While waiting to see what would come out of the conversations between the clones, Cylia, intrigued, questioned Sulas.

- Why don't we ask Kenneth's clone and have him answer directly? Why don't we just ask him if he has any enemies, for example?

Sulas sighed slightly before answering.

- It's not that simple. What we're looking for is a weak signal, something difficult to detect. If it were that obvious, Kenneth himself would have known about it and escaped his fate. We can't ask the clone to do what Kenneth couldn't do. My algorithm is based on learning by imitation, nothing more. Technically, it would be possible to create an improved clone by setting other objectives during the learning process, but that would take time we don't have.

Cylia frowned, trying to follow Sulas's explanation. Curiosity was getting the better of her confusion.

- Sulas, I've been hearing about algorithms everywhere for years, but I've never understood what they are exactly. Can you explain it to me simply, as if I were a ten-year-old child, please?

Sulas smiled, ready to popularize a concept seen as complex yet simple in reality.

- Ah, my dear Cylia, it's not that complicated. An algorithm is a series of steps designed to perform a task or solve a problem. Think of it as a recipe. On a computer, it's much the same thing, a sequence of instructions programmed with computer code. You could also think of it as a musical phrase, where the notes are replaced by codes that the computer can execute.

- And with that alone, we arrive at artificial intelligence? asked Cylia, visibly surprised.

- Exactly! replied Sulas. In music, when you start superimposing several instruments, each with its own notes, you get complex compositions like a symphony. In computing, it's similar, but you have to imagine thousands of instruments combined. It's the same principle, but on a much larger scale.

Cylia nodded, fascinated.

Dihya listened attentively to the conversation and wanted to add something to the answer given by Sulas.

- You, the AI expert, know where the term "algorithm" comes from?

Sulas rolled his eyes.

- Dihya, please don't start.

- Go on, make an effort, Dihya insisted, laughing.

- We don't have time for that.

- Well, if it's any consolation, you're not the only one of your kind who doesn't know, far from it, said Dihya. In fact, at an AI trade show I attended a few months ago, I did a little test on the subject. Every time I passed a stand, I played naive and asked the question about the definition of an algorithm and the origin of the word. To this second question, none of these AI geniuses could answer me!

Sulas sighed before pressing a button on his watch and leaning over to talk up close.

- Atlas, can you tell me the origin of the term algorithm?

Atlas was a chatbot that Sulas had built himself to run on his own machines, not in the cloud. He had given it the name in reference to the Atlas Mountains, to which people of previous generations would turn with wishes and other requests. This was the case for young women whose husbands had been exiled abroad, usually to France, to ensure their safe return. The echo sent back by the mountain symbolized the response and showed that the call had been heard beyond the sea.

- But you're cheating, said Dihya to Sulas.

- Of course not, Atlas is my assistant, I trained him. I'm his creator!

- AI isn't called "machine learning" for nothing. He probably knows, but you don't.

- Well, OK, will you let us listen to the answer now?

Sulas transferred the sound to the large speaker in the office so that Cylia and Dihya could hear the answer. A clear, articulate voice emanated from the speaker.

=================================

Deepfake

🔊 The term "algorithm" derives from Muḥammad ibn Mûsâ al-Khwârizmî, an eminent Persian mathematician, astronomer and geographer whose contributions have shaped the evolution of mathematics and science around the world. Born in 780 A.D. in the Khwarezm region of present-day Uzbekistan, once part of the Persian Empire, al-Khwârizmî spent much of his life in Baghdad.

In Baghdad, he joined the prestigious House of Wisdom (Bayt al-Hikma), a renowned center of learning and translation. Nicknamed the "father of algebra", Al-Khwārizmī is the author of the "Kitāb al-Mukhtaṣar fī ḥisāb al-jabr wa'l-muqābala", a pioneering treatise that lays the foundations for solving linear and quadratic equations. A single copy of this Arabic manuscript has survived and is preciously preserved at Oxford University. The word "algebra" itself derives from the word "al-jabr" in the title, meaning "reduction of a fracture" in Arabic.

One of Al-Khwârizmî's major works, "Kitâb al-ḥisâb al-hindî" or "Book of Indian Arithmetic", introduced the decimal system and numerals used around the world today. This treatise was translated into Latin under the title "Algoritmi de numero Indorum", from which the modern term "algorithm" derives.

To honor his contributions to astronomy, two asteroids and an impact crater on the far side of the Moon are named after Al-Khwārizmī. It's a testament to the lasting impact of his work on the world of science and mathematics.

= =

As soon as the chatbot fell silent, Dihya was startled out of her thoughts. Wide-eyed, she turned to Sulas.

- You see? This gentleman is the father of algebra! You know, that discipline which is the basis of all the formulas you use to build your AI algos, she said with palpable excitement in her voice. None of you code geniuses have named a single AI model after this great man.

Sulas, sitting opposite Dihya, burst out laughing, his humor always present even at the most unexpected moments.

- Are you going to repeat what Atlas just told us? He's already said it all, hasn't he?

Dihya didn't let herself be distracted and continued on her way, determined to see her thought through to the end.

- Have you heard? Al-jabr is the term Al-Khwârizmî used to describe transformations to reduce or simplify mathematical formulas. The word originally meant "to reduce the fracture".

Sulas nodded, smiling.

- Yes, that's right, I heard you right, he replied, emphasizing each word.

Dihya, still deep in thought, continued with a twinkle in her eye.

- Does this term ring a bell?

- No, nothing.

- You know, there used to be no hospitals. In the villages, there was what's called a healer, a person who treated sprained or dislocated limbs. This person also knew how to apply a splint after a fracture. One of my father's aunts was the village specialist. People flocked to her for the slightest health problem. As a little anecdote, from what my father told me, she sometimes managed to cure people for whom no doctor had a remedy. But what I really wanted to tell you about was the term used in Berber for this splint.

Sulas, intrigued, leaned forward slightly.

- Yes, which term?

- Well, quite simply *tujbirth*, a Berberized form of the Arabic verb *tujbir*, from which the name *al-jabr* is derived.

Just as Dihya finished uttering these words, a continuous beep sounded in the distance, breaking the studious atmosphere of the room. A red alarm appeared on the clone conversation control screen. The air instantly became heavy with tension.

Sulas rushed to the screen, his fingers flying over the controls, ready to interrupt anything if necessary.

- Houston, we've got a problem! he exclaimed.

Chapter 81

While Dihya and Sulas were busy getting Asklepios, Kenneth's clone, to talk to them, trying to find out the truth about the tragedy that had claimed Kenneth's life, Tarakna wasn't missing a thing. He was watching everything on his control screens, his eyes fixed on the data streams that scrolled by at dizzying speed. A worried wrinkle crossed his forehead.

He soon realized that someone had managed to automate the exchanges, creating a deepfake of Dihya. The precision of the imitation was formidable: every gesture, every intonation of the voice was reproduced to perfection. Tarakna felt a surge of anger mixed with admiration. Until now, he had thought he was the only one to possess this unique skill. This new revelation made him realize that he had a worthy adversary.

The aim of this maneuver was clear to him: to gather as much information as possible about Kenneth, and eventually uncover the truth about his suicide. The enigmatic Kenneth had left behind more questions than answers, and Asklepios was the key.

For Tarakna, the choice of unplugging Asklepios to put an end to this intrusion was a trivial option. But Tarakna was a gambler at heart. Faced with this provocation, he made a paradoxical decision. Instead of unplugging the chatbot, he decided to increase the computing power dedicated to it. The processors revved up, the fans humming like a beehive in fury. The speed of exchanges increased exponentially, and in an instant, Sulas's server was flooded with an astronomical amount of data.

Chapter 82

Sulas, assailed by a sudden wave of information, struggled to make sense of it all. His fingers flew across the keyboard, while his eyes stared intently at the scrolling lines of code. Dihya, anxious, tried to make sense of the situation.

- What's going on? Can you explain?

- As you know, just an hour ago, we were trying to increase the exchange rate. Now, inexplicably, the throughput is too high and we're receiving too much information. The designer seems to want to overwhelm us to prevent us from processing the data. Too much information kills information!

Dihya, having grasped what was at stake, proposed a solution.

- We could reduce the speed on our side. Kenneth's clone won't be able to keep up with us. We set the pace, don't we?

- It's clever, but it's the easy way out. Remember, we wanted to get as much information as possible in the first place.

Dihya understood that Sulas was facing a dilemma and didn't want to take the easy way out. After a few minutes of intense reflection, he abruptly rose from his chair.

- Humans can't read too quickly or assimilate too much information at once, but AI can.

- What do you mean? asked Dihya.

- I think we should maintain the current pace of exchanges, but I'll transfer the results to Atlas for pre-processing. It will summarize ten minutes of conversation for us at each iteration. I'll configure the output size to be readable in about one minute. In this way, we'll divide the throughput by ten without losing crucial information. That's what I'm hoping for, and I'm counting on Atlas to deliver accurate summaries.

- Excellent idea, replies Dihya with satisfaction. That's what ministers do, they ask their assistants for summary sheets instead of reading long reports.

Sulas, concentrating on his task, barely heard Dihya's words. His fingers were frantically hitting the keys on the keyboard, producing lines of code at breakneck speed. After a few minutes, he looked up.

- It's ready, he announced, pointing the mouse at his right-hand screen. Dihya, you'll read the summaries posted here. The essentials will normally be there. Atlas will do the job! Cylia, for you, it'll be on that left-hand screen. Atlas has already started summarizing the data received so far. He'll do this in sections, of course. Now it's your turn!

Sulas breathed a huge sigh of relief before dropping into his armchair, closing his eyes to try and clear his mind and relax.

Chapter 83

Kenneth, an enigma, dissected under the insistent gazes of Dihya and Cylia, the incessant stream of questions and discussions with his clone having rendered him almost transparent. They now knew every significant detail of his life, digitized and stored in the meanders of the AI. But this intrusion wasn't limited to Kenneth. Dihya, whose life had also opened up like a book before Cylia, was suffering the same consequences.

In a moment of respite, Cylia turned to Dihya.

- You know, I had no idea that screen addiction could be so serious. Did you really go to Crete to disconnect? I'm glued to my phone from morning to night and I don't see the problem. I even sleep with it, like a blanket!

Exhausted by the continuous onslaught of information on her screen, Dihya replied laconically out of respect for the friend who had come to help her.

- What do you want me to say? If this life suits you, go on.

Realizing that Dihya was in no mood to prolong the conversation, Cylia returned to her screen, resuming her reading and notes.

As the discussions progressed, new avenues began to emerge, ready to be explored in depth. This required time and, above all, rigorous organization. While waiting for the next report, Dihya, resuming her role as investigative journalist, got up and stood in front of a whiteboard.

- We need a methodical approach, like real investigators, to get to the bottom of this case. The motives behind a crime may vary, but some are common to all.

Dihya wrote the main motifs on the blackboard:

    1. Financial gain

    2. Personal conflicts

3. Thrill/Excitement

4. Revenge

5. Substance abuse

6. Mental health problems

7. Social influence

8. Opportunism

Then she explained them succinctly:

1. Financial gain: Many crimes are committed in order to obtain money or valuable goods.

2. Personal conflicts: Some crimes arise from personal conflicts or disputes between individuals.

3. Thrill or Excitement: For some individuals, the thrill of breaking the law or engaging in risky behavior is the primary motive.

4. Revenge or retaliation: Some crimes are committed out of revenge or retaliation for perceived wrongs or injustices.

5. Substance abuse: Addiction to drugs or alcohol can lead individuals to commit crimes in order to obtain money for drugs or to support their addiction.

6. Mental health problems: People suffering from mental health problems may commit crimes because of their condition.

7. Social influence: Some individuals may commit crimes because of peer pressure or social influences, especially within gangs.

8. Opportunism: Sometimes crimes are committed simply because the opportunity presents itself, as in burglary, theft or fraud.

K

Dihya completed her presentation with rigorous professionalism:

- These motives often intersect. We need to identify each key piece of information as a potential motive and examine it in detail. This rigor is essential to avoid confusing the issue.

She stared intently at her friends, aware that their success depended on their ability to be methodical and concentrated in unravelling a web of rare complexity.

Chapter 84

Her eyes heavy with fatigue, Dihya made coffee after coffee to stay awake. Dawn was approaching, and she could barely make out the words on her screen after hours of reading. Even so, she tried to organize her research.

- In light of what we know about Kenneth and the information we've gathered so far, we can already rule out several possible motives, she said, listing:

    1. ~~Financial gain~~

    2. Personal conflicts

    3. Thrill/Excitement

    4. Revenge

    5. ~~Substance abuse~~

    6. ~~Mental health problems~~

    7. ~~Social influence~~

    8. ~~Opportunism~~

- Are you okay with that? she asked, trying to make sure she wasn't overlooking anything.

Cylia spoke first.

- I agree. Looking at Kenneth's past, I'd lean more towards a personal conflict, but we'll see as we go along.

Sulas then intervened.

- Given the behavior of the clone designer, I wouldn't be surprised if Kenneth simply fell into the wrong place at the wrong time. The guy behind it all seems motivated by the thrill. You can see it in the way he acts.

Dihya continued, explaining her findings.

- I must admit I was a bit surprised. Kenneth claimed to have had only three or four female conquests, but he had at least double that number. Although most of these relationships didn't last, the one that intrigues me is a certain Elisa Klein. They met at university and stayed together for eight years. A separation after such a long relationship is never trivial.

Sulas, attentive, couldn't help thinking that Dihya, because of her relationship with Kenneth, was perhaps not the most objective person for this investigation. Perhaps she was letting jealousy get the better of her, focusing too much on Kenneth's former conquests. He preferred to keep his doubts to himself and continued to listen.

- I did some research on the Internet and found some interesting information about Elisa. She became a lawyer like Kenneth and lives in the South, in Saint-Raphaël, near Nice. According to her Instagram, she leads a dream life and has been dating a famous actor for two years. She seems to live in another world.

- From what I understand, intervened Sulas, Kenneth lived for a long time with another woman with whom he had a daughter. I don't think that's necessary. Do you have anything else?

- Yes, replied Dihya. The second person on my list is a certain Michael Klaus. He was a colleague with whom Kenneth had opened his first practice. Kenneth had lent him money for a real estate project, but Michael never paid it back. They quarreled and Kenneth left the firm to open another. I found some heated exchanges between them.

- It's already more interesting, said Sulas impatiently.

- But this story is a little dated. Michael has emigrated to Israel and built up a real estate empire. His business is doing well, he's rich and has no reason to hold a grudge against Kenneth. He could have hired someone to get even, but I don't think so. Kenneth hasn't mentioned this gentleman in any of his messages since their separation.

- It remains an interesting avenue, although I still think the designer has to be motivated by a personal motive, added Sulas. Using deepfakes requires considerable motivation. Money alone wouldn't be enough.

- I agree. Let's not rule it out. Now let's move on to what seems to me to be the most serious lead. Kenneth managed to get a client acquitted in a serious murder case. The man was accused of killing his wife in a hotel room after a violent argument. The evidence was overwhelming, but Kenneth managed to exonerate him. The victim's family never accepted the verdict, and Kenneth received threatening letters. He even filed a complaint, fearing for his and his daughter's safety. That was about a year ago. So, it's relatively recent, and perhaps related to our...

Cylia stopped Dihya in her tracks to share a piece of information that had particularly caught her attention.

- Kenneth received an incredible amount of hate mail after his book was published a few months ago. I didn't get to read them all, but there was one that particularly struck me. Some messages congratulated him, others insulted or threatened him, but this one was different. It was sent from a rather strange e-mail address:

taraka1984@yopmail.com

Sulas, exhausted and still slumped in his armchair, gasped at this detail.

- Did you say yopmail? he asked eagerly.

- Yes, that's right. Have a look.

Sulas straightened up, looking suddenly interested.

- This is known as a disposable e-mail address. It's often used by criminals to leave no trace. It's like making a call from a public phone booth and paying in cash. It leaves almost no trace. Please show me.

Cylia turned her screen so that Sulas could see what was displayed.

From: tarakna1984@yopmail.com

Subject: Right of reply

Hi Kenneth,

You have protected Satan and cast a veil over his hell.

The thunderbolts of the gods will fall on you and you will suffer for the rest of your life.

- TARAKNA -

K
- -

Sulas turned to Dihya and Cylia to share his thoughts.

- It's supposed to be a right of reply. That's what you do after a publication in a newspaper, he explained, looking at Cylia.

Dihya is no stranger to this mechanism. A newspaper opens its columns for a right of reply when a person or organization believes that information published about them is inaccurate, defamatory or injurious to their honor or reputation. The right of reply is a legal mechanism enabling this person or organization to rectify the information.

- So, this person disagrees with some of the facts published by Kenneth in his book? asked Cylia.

- Yes, but can you decipher this mysterious e-mail to understand the subject? Not me, anyway. It looks like it's from a symbology fan or a member of a secret cult. I don't know anything about it. Dihya, doesn't it speak to you?

Dihya was sitting on the ground, exhausted, and struggling to get up. Sulas went to help her to her feet. She leaned over the screen to read the message. A moment later, a mixture of astonishment and terror invaded her face.

Chapter 85

The mail was full of mystery and imbued with a palpable menace. The phrase "The thunderbolt of the gods will strike you and you will suffer for the rest of your life" echoed relentlessly in Dihya's mind. She turned to Sulas with an urgent question.

- Can we find occurrences of this email address in Kenneth's data?

- Not directly, but Kenneth's clone, which has been trained on his personal data, could provide us with this information, or at least something close to it, replied Sulas. Let's give it a try.

Sulas wrote his request to the chatbot, and the response came almost immediately. The first thing the clone sent back was a short, signed text, originally written on a letter and photographed by Kenneth using his phone. In the eyes of the three friends, the message left no doubt as to its threatening intentions towards the recipient, presumably Kenneth.

> *"I follow you everywhere. You forgot something."*

- TARAKNA -

Tarakna, who knew better than anyone that photos could contain information crucial to the clones' performance, had set up a database for this purpose. Each photo retrieved from Kenneth's phone was processed by an AI to provide a detailed description of its contents. During a discussion with the clone, he could access this database and extract information useful for his answers. It was thanks to this mechanism that the threatening mail was returned by the chatbot at Sulas' request.

On the same principle, the clone also sent back three messages found in Kenneth's email box: the one Cylia had come across, as well as two others exchanged with a different address:

arachne@gmail.com

The first e-mail had been sent to Kenneth a few days before the woman was murdered in his office. It was a confirmation of an appointment between a client and the lawyer. The second e-mail concerned the sending of a file, just after this appointment, to start legal proceedings.

Sulas, slightly surprised by the result, expressed his feelings.

- I wasn't expecting that answer at all. The two email addresses aren't that similar, are they? One is "arachne" and the other "tarakna"!

As Dihya replayed over and over again the phrase "The thunderbolt of the gods will fall upon you...", an illumination struck her.

- Of course it does. It all makes sense. Do you know what Arachne is?

A smile appeared on Cylia's face, as she had a passion for mythology.

- It's the character from Greek mythology who excelled in the art of weaving and was transformed into a spider by the goddess Athena, Cylia replied confidently.

- Exactly, Cylia! And that's the symbol you see displayed at the bottom of the first e-mail, a spider.

Just as Sulas was about to interrupt, Dihya continued at once.

- And the two main words in the emails correspond quite well and mean almost the same thing. Sulas, can you ask Atlas for the definition of the word "tarakna"?

Sulas nodded before making the request to his watch. The chatbot delivered its answer through the office speakers.

===================================

"Yes, of course. Tarakna is a Berber word used in North Africa. Its meaning may vary slightly from region to region, but it refers to much the same object: a large, beautiful woven woolen cloth. It's used either as a bed cover to keep warm in winter, or as a decorative rug to cover a floor or wall."

===================================

Sulas restarted the chatbot, his curiosity piqued.

- And is there a connection between the words "Tarakna" and "Arachne"?

The response was instantaneous.

=================================

🔊 "Absolutely. The Berber word "tarakna" has the root "arakna", because the initial "t" is nothing other than the feminine determiner, the equivalent of "la" in French. It is also sometimes added at the end of a word to reinforce its feminine character. For example, we say "amazigh" to designate a man and "tamazight" for a woman. As Berber and Greek civilizations are closely intertwined, there is a common origin for these two words, belonging to the same semantic field."

=================================

To convince her friends once and for all, Dihya asked Atlas about the origin of the French word "tisser". The answer was equally enlightening:

=================================

🔊 This verb comes from the Latin "texo" and its ancient Greek equivalent "tékhné", meaning "skill" or "art".

=================================

Dihya used this information to strengthen her argument.

- And guess what they call a spider in Berber? Quite simply "tissist", which of course recalls weaving [Tisser]!

- Everything fits together, acknowledged Sulas, visibly impressed.

- Whoever is behind these emails is mysterious and cunning. We need to contact him to see what he has to say, suggested Dihya.

- Forget the first email address, it's disposable and he probably doesn't use it anymore, added Sulas.

- Yes, I understood that. We'll contact him on the second address, Gmail, and see if that gets us anywhere.

Just as Dihya was about to return to her post, Cylia called out to her.

- Dihya, could you please tell us more about Berber mythology, which you obviously know well?

- I'll do it later, but not now. Sorry, we don't have time, replied Dihya kindly. Here, I'll show you a video in the meantime. Scan this QR code.

As Cylia pointed her phone at the code, Sulas breathed a sigh of relief. He knew that Dihya would be hard to stop once she started explaining.

As Dihya headed for her chair, she thought again of Cylia. It was she who had put them on this promising track. Her unique perspective, far removed from the scholastic method she had expounded, and despite any prejudices she might have had against her, had enabled their investigation to move forward. Diversity, so dear to Dihya, was reinforced in her mind even more after this episode.

Chapter 86

As a seasoned investigative journalist, Dihya didn't rush to broach the main subject with Tarakna, preferring the subtle foot-in-the-door strategy to build trust first. She requested an interview under the pretext of investigating AI advances, leaving the true nature of her inquiry veiled. Revealing her real identity was a risk: Tarakna would recognize her immediately. She therefore opted for a new e-mail address created for the occasion and a brand-new telephone, knowing that she was being spied on on her usual device.

It was a long wait for an answer. Tarakna showed a willingness to answer her questions. Dihya sent him a first series of questions, including one on deepfakes: "Do you think that one day we'll be faced with perfect, undetectable deepfakes?"

Tarakna's reply made her jump: "You're living proof that this is possible. Despite your caution, you were never able to detect Asklepios."

Dihya discovered for the first time the nickname given by Tarakna to Kenneth's clone: Asclepius, "he who revives the dead". Above all, she understood that Tarakna knew he was corresponding with her, Dihya. But how had he guessed her identity? Had he hacked into her new device? Impossible, she thought, for she had used it exclusively for these exchanges. Nor could any attached files have infected the device, since there were none. Total incomprehension overwhelmed her.

There was only one solution left for Dihya to unravel this mystery: ask her friend Sulas for help. She called him. A moment later, he picked up.

- Hello Dihya, how are you?

- Hi Sulas, I'm fine, but I have a question for you.

- Yes, what?

- I contacted Tarakna using a new phone and a newly created Skype account. He guessed it was me. How could he?

- Several hypotheses. Remember when we interviewed Kenneth's clone...

Dihya interrupted him.

- He calls him Asclepius, the clone, just so you know.

- OK, interesting, still into symbols and mysteries. Anyway, for your question: the first possibility is that he was monitoring our exchanges with Asclepius and made the connection with your request. The other is that, like you, he's using an exclusive email for this affair.

- I think you're right. I'm leaning towards the second hypothesis. By avoiding using an address that can be traced on the Internet, you make it harder to trace your real identity.

- Exactly. An email address used for something else can be shared and resold by data brokers, making it easier to correlate data and identify the individual.

- Great, thanks Sulas. You're a lifesaver. See you soon.

Sulas was about to hang up, but remembered something.

- Hang on a sec. Now that you're on the trail of the villain behind the Kenneth case, can I shut down everything on my machines and delete the clone?

- Do you mean to say that it is permanently deleted and can no longer be used?

- Yes.

- Not so fast, please. We'll keep the clone for a while yet, so it can tell us more about the case.

Dihya, clearly starting to get attached to Kenneth's clone, lost the thread of the discussion.

- I'm talking about your clone; Kenneth's is under Tarakna's control, I remind you, clarified Sulas.

- Oh, yes, that's right. You can delete my clone. He's no use to us anymore and I don't want him out there. Delete! Delete!

- Noted. Good luck, Dihya.

- Thanks for everything, Sulas. See you soon.

Dihya hung up and took a deep breath. She now had to rethink her strategy with Tarakna. Knowing that he knew her identity, she had no choice but to get straight to the point and try to wring the truth out of him.

Chapter 87

After a series of direct, straightforward exchanges, Dihya plucked up the courage to offer Tarakna an interview via Skype. Aware of the risk she was taking - that of Tarakna cutting off all contact and losing track of him forever - she had no option but to go for it.

From then on, Dihya never took her eyes off her mailbox, watching for the slightest notification with growing tension. Every sound from her phone set her heart racing.

Two days later, the silence was finally broken by a brief sound on her phone. Dihya felt her heart race. Glancing at the screen, she saw the long-awaited message from Tarakna. She trembled nervously as she slid her finger across the screen, her clammy hand making the operation hazardous. After several attempts, she finally managed to open the message. As she read the contents, her face lit up with a glow of triumph. Tarakna's reply, though brief and enigmatic, opened a door to deliverance, to truth.

From: arachne@gmail.com

Subject: RE: Interview proposal

I accept. See you tonight at 10 (Skype: tarkna1984)

*"O folle Aragne, sì vedea io te
già mezza ragna, trista in su li stracci
de l'opera che mal per te si fé."*

- Tarakna -

Dihya was ecstatic to discover the long-awaited answer. Tarakna had agreed to talk on Skype and had even provided her with his pseudonym to find him. Heart pounding and hands trembling, she immediately opened the Skype application and launched the search. A number appeared, accompanied by a profile photo of a spider. Bingo!

Her joy was short-lived, however. One detail was worrying her. At the bottom of Tarakna's message, a sentence written in a strange language, similar to Italian or Latin, hammered at the back of her mind. What sense could it make? Determined not to leave anything to chance, Dihya decided she had to understand this riddle before making the call. You can never be too careful...

Chapter 88

Dihya stood frozen in front of her computer screen, staring at the message, trying to unravel its mystery. The foreign words composing it formed an insoluble enigma in her eyes:

> "O folle Aragne, sì vedea io te
> già mezza ragna, trista in su li stracci
> de l'opera che mal per te si fé."

She tried to decipher them. She positioned and analyzed each translated word, trying to deduce an overall meaning:

crazy - spider - reign - sad - opera - evil

After long minutes of fruitless wrestling with this esoteric text, she finally gave in to the easy way out. She took a photo of the message and sent it to ChatGPT, asking for an explanation. Renowned for its extraordinary character recognition capabilities, the chatbot responded almost instantly, with surgical precision:

===============================

🔊 Of course. Here's an explanation of the text you provided:

This passage, taken from Purgatory (Canto XII, verses 43-45) of Dante Alighieri's Divine Comedy, refers to the Greek myth of Arachne. Written in medieval Tuscan, it can be translated as follows: "O mad Arachne, I could already see you half spider, sad on the tatters of the work you made for your misfortune."

Dante recalls the tragic fate of Arachne, a talented weaver who, out of pride, challenged the goddess Athena to a weaving contest. To punish her, Athena turned her into a spider. The poet describes her at the moment of her metamorphosis, half-human half-spider, sadly contemplating the remains of her destroyed tapestry.

This powerful image serves as an example of the dangers of pride and presumption in the face of divine authority, a central theme of Purgatory. Dante uses this mythological reference to illustrate the harmful consequences of human arrogance, inviting the reader to meditate on humility and respect for the divine order.

==================================

The answer was a revelation for Dihya. Although she knew Dante's works, she had not made the connection with Tarakna's text. Suddenly, everything became clearer.

***

Dante's *Purgatorio*, the second part of the Divine Comedy after *Inferno*, offers an optimistic moral perspective on human nature and the process of redemption. It teaches that everyone is capable of improving despite their weaknesses, through a gradual process of introspection, repentance and personal effort. The work emphasizes the importance of individual responsibility, while at the same time valuing community support in the quest for moral perfection. Purgatory illustrates a balance between divine justice and mercy, showing that although the path to virtue is difficult, it is accessible to all who are willing to acknowledge their faults and work to overcome them. Ultimately, Dante presents us with a vision of humanity capable of transformation and spiritual elevation, offering a message of hope and redemption.

***

By including an extract from Purgatory, Tarakna wanted to show Dihya that, after playing with the fire of hell, he was on the road to redemption, ready to face up to his faults and finally hope for peace and paradise. Deep inside him, the same symbolic leitmotif recurred once again: *"I elevate myself by rising above myself."*

Dihya screamed with all her might, a cry of deliverance, perhaps even the opening to the truth about Kenneth's disappearance. She couldn't hold back her words, spoken in a deep voice:

- I've got you now, you bastard, she triumphed. Behind every technology, there's a man, and in every man, there are flaws.

Dihya turned off her computer, then threw herself onto the sofa. She closed her eyes, already imagining tonight's 10 p.m. Skype chat.

Chapter 89

It was 9:55pm. Dihya was on edge. She paced nervously around the living room of her house, trying to fend off the unbearable wait. Impatience was gnawing at her, she couldn't wait to hear what Tarakna was going to say.

The clock was ticking: ten seconds. She fixed her phone on a stand, next to a recorder already running to capture every word of the conversation to come, if Tarakna didn't change his mind at the last minute.

At 10 p.m. sharp, Dihya pressed the "call" button and waited. The tone echoed in the oppressive silence, but nobody picked up. She repeated the operation a second time. Still nothing. Five minutes passed, and she began to worry. What if Tarakna decided to call it off and cut all ties for good? A thousand scenarios raced through her mind, each more alarming than the last. Impatience was her Achilles' heel, and she couldn't stand still.

She stood up to walk a little, hoping to calm her agitation, when suddenly the ringing of a Skype call broke the silence. Her heart raced. She ran to sit down again and picked up the phone.

A masked face, reminiscent of Anonymous, appeared on the screen.

- Hello, Dihya, I'm sorry I'm late, Tarakna apologized in a hoarse voice.

- Hello, Tarakna, don't worry, it happens.

- Thank you for the invitation.

- I'd like to thank you for agreeing to answer my interview, retorted Dihya.

The cordial tone of the discussion, detached from everything that had happened, hardly surprised Dihya. It was the usual attitude of criminals in front of a microphone. Good, she thought, he'd feel freer to talk.

And so it was. Tarakna answered all Dihya's questions with disconcerting frankness. Dihya was pleasantly surprised and encouraged him to go ahead.

- Tarakna, thank you for your honesty. However, I'm still not sure why you're wearing that mask. For someone seeking to atone for his sins, isn't it paradoxical?

- No, I was waiting for you to ask. I would have taken it off in the first minute if you'd asked. I want to get to heaven, but I'd rather be guided there.

Dihya was taken aback by this answer, imbued with symbolism. It reminded her of Dante climbing the mountain of Purgatory, accompanied at every step by a guide.

As her mind wandered through the meanders of The Divine Comedy, her interlocutor suddenly removed his mask. Dihya gasped. She found herself face to face with the man who had turned her life into a living hell. The scene was surreal.

- As promised, I'm out in the open. I have nothing more to hide from you, added Tarakna.

Dihya was speechless. She stared at this angelic face, difficult to associate with a criminal, reminiscent of Julian Assange's, except for one detail: a tattoo in the shape of letter "P" adorned his forehead.

For Dihya, an enthusiast of Dante's work, this detail came as no surprise. She returned to her memories of the *Purgatorio*.

***

Purgatory, like an inverted reflection of Hell, rises not as an abyss, but as a majestic mountain. Here, the order of sins is reversed: Dante's journey begins with the heaviest burdens, Pride, and ends with the lightest, Lust.

Each cornice of this spiritual ascent is protected by a guardian angel, symbolizing a virtue: humility, charity, peace, zeal, justice, temperance and chastity. On each level, penitent souls are confronted with representations of their vice and the opposite virtue, a visual and spiritual lesson to help them purify themselves.

Having reached the threshold of the terrestrial Paradise, Virgil, the faithful guide, has to give up his place. Dante is then taken in charge by the Latin poet Stace, who leads him into the celestial garden where Matelda welcomes him, foreshadowing the long-awaited appearance of Beatrice (the woman Dante fell in love with but never had the chance to marry).

Souls in Purgatory are already promised salvation, but before entering Paradise, they must climb this mountain, reminiscent of the pilgrims of yesteryear who, in a fit of penitence, made their way to Rome or Santiago de Compostela. Each soul must cross each cornice, purifying itself of the corresponding sins. On this journey, Dante encounters souls marked by their most significant sin, placing them in an intimate setting representative of their earthly lives.

Purgatory serves as a place of atonement, and Dante himself bears the stigmata of this purification: the guardian angel of Purgatory has seven "P's" engraved on his forehead, symbolizing the deadly sins. At the end of each cornice, the angel erases a "P" with his wing, marking the end of atonement for that sin.

***

Dihya realized that Tarakna had reached the final stage of his purification process. There was just one last sin to erase before he reached the summit of the mountain, his *Paradiso*. She calmly asked him to tell her the whole story and what had led him to attack Kenneth. Tarakna took his time, meticulously detailing every step of the way and the motives behind his actions. He repeatedly insisted that Kenneth's death had never been part of his plan. He even declared himself ready to testify in court to exonerate Kenneth from the murder of which he was accused.

After the detailed account of events, Dihya couldn't help but think back to the story of the Clockwork Orange. Ironically, Kenneth, who had told her the story, had himself become Alex, transformed into an automaton by psychological torture, albeit of a new kind. The only difference was that Kenneth wasn't lucky enough to survive his suicide attempt, unlike Alex DeLarge.

At the same time, Dihya, in the grip of a sort of Stockholm syndrome, found herself feeling pity for Tarakna. She finally understood the true meaning of his nickname. Tarakna, meaning "woven cloth", evoked a simple object intended for protection, but whose intricate design made it a piece of great value. Its presence embellished a wall, but also served as a reminder of the imperfections it concealed. Like the man behind the pseudonym, the canvas was merely a façade masking the fragility of a man whom life had not spared.

At the end of the Skype discussion, Dihya felt an immense sense of relief. She now had all the explanations and evidence she needed to exonerate Kenneth. He could finally rest in peace, and she, freed from a huge burden, could turn the page and move on with her life.

Replaying the events in her mind, Dihya became fully aware of the crucial role Kenneth's tattoo had played in the outcome of the affair. This symbol, silent witness to the deep love that united them, had shed light on what would otherwise have remained forever obscure. She knew that some might consider her a chauvinist, but if it hadn't been for that long, intense conversation she'd had with Kenneth about her roots, he'd never have had the idea of engraving this tribute on his skin. The fabric of human history seemed to him like an inextricably knotted rope, each knot containing a secret, each ending facilitating another. This image lingered in Dihya's mind as she made her way, exhausted, to her bed. Her long conversation with Tarakna had drained her of strength, and the clock was already well past midnight.

Chapter 90

Night enveloped Paris in its dark mantle. Dihya, Sulas and Cylia had met at a café in the Latin Quarter, a familiar place where they hoped to take stock of the whole affair. Dihya, full of pride, launched into an account of her long discussions with Tarakna a few days earlier. She told them how she'd managed to get him to talk, and above all how he'd agreed to testify at the upcoming trial to clear Kenneth of all charges against him. She even began to imagine the consequences of the whole story, the scenario in her mind already forming an outline for her next article in the Herald:

- I bet there'll be a before and after to the Kenneth affair, she said, her tone alarmist. Videoconferencing will be banned in some companies, which could have a devastating effect on the economy if a Covid19-style crisis occurs. The same will apply to the judicial use of digital media as evidence. Even video surveillance could be called into question.

Sulas tried to add a nuance:

- There will certainly be stricter supervision. Every piece of evidence will have to pass under the forks of security and AI experts. A complete audit of the absence of manipulation will have to be presented at the same time as the evidence.

Dihya, somewhat offended, completed her remarks:

- Yes, but who will pay all these costs? Private individuals? Such an audit would cost a fortune. The justice system? It's already in its death throes. What I see instead is a terrifying world in which inequalities will grow as never before. The rich and powerful will create alibis based on deepfakes to exonerate themselves, while the rest will suffer.

- I confess that this prospect frightens me too, added Sulas.

A heavy silence settled around the table. Cylia, who had been listening attentively until then, finally spoke up.

- He is mysterious, this Tarakna. All the symbols he uses are strange. With this story, he may have wanted to show off his power or, on the contrary, warn the world about the great danger of these deepfakes.

- I'd go for the second hypothesis, replied Dihya. Showing a certain power, yes, but it's probably a facade. He's probably more vulnerable than he looks.

- Technically, what he's done is pretty impressive, added Sulas. To build two clones simultaneously and have them interact live is remarkable. We've all seen the quality of Kenneth's clone. Even you, Dihya, who know him well, were impressed.

Cylia, curious, seized the opportunity.

- Is Kenneth's clone still active? she asked, looking at Dihya.

Answering yes meant admitting to continuing to speak with the clone. Dihya paused before breaking the silence.

- In any case, Tarakna told me he would only deactivate it if I asked him to. I haven't said anything to him about it yet. For my part, I've decided not to continue these virtual discussions. Without physical contact, I just can't do it. I've done my mourning and I want to move on. But one question haunts me: is it right to keep this clone alive?

- Why? asked Sulas, surprised.

- It's about Kenneth's mother. She still doesn't know he's dead, and no one dares tell her. She's very ill and her heart surely couldn't take the shock of learning the truth. I wonder if it wouldn't be better to keep the clone active for her, so she can continue to talk with him on Skype and believe he's alive. Surely Tarakna would agree. But is it morally acceptable?

Silence fell over the table. Sulas and Cylia were deep in thought. Dihya, her face darkened, continued.

- Frankly, I don't know what to do.

Sulas spoke up.

- It's a moral dilemma. To reveal the truth to his mother at the risk of killing her, or to hide her son's death from her... I don't know either.

Cylia in turn expressed her opinion.

- Personally, if I were in the mother's shoes, I'd rather know the truth, even if it killed me. What's life like after losing a son, especially at her age? Imagine if she found out differently and then saw him on Skype? She'd lose her mind.

- A priori, she wouldn't call her son on Skype if she knew he was dead, retorted Sulas. But you're right, you never know.

Dihya listened attentively to her friends before sighing.

- You're right, we must respect the mother's rights. After all, death is part of life. I don't have to get involved in this clone business. It's ruined my life enough. I won't say anything to Kenneth's lawyer. He'll inform his mother when he deems it necessary. It must be difficult for him, but he must be used to breaking this kind of news. Come what may.

Night was well advanced in Paris. Cylia had to catch the metro and couldn't stay any longer. The three friends embraced before parting, each heading off in a different direction.

As she walked to her car, Dihya was already thinking about the impending trial. Anything could happen, and this was her last battle before finally turning this sad page in her life.

Chapter 91

The Kenneth case was widely covered by the tabloids and news magazines. The courtroom at the Paris Tribunal was packed. Rows of patinated wooden chairs were occupied by scoop-hungry journalists, onlookers who had come for the frenzy of courtroom drama, and relatives supporting one side or the other. The atmosphere was charged with palpable tension, every whisper, every movement amplifying the nervous anticipation.

On one side of the room, Mr. Morlon, the young lawyer for the plaintiff, stood alone in the box. Unfortunately, none of the victim's family had come forward, as they had throughout the investigation. The only witnesses he was able to call were one of Kenneth's neighbors and his ex-wife.

Mr. Morlon leafed through his file with intense concentration, aware of the solidity of the evidence he possessed. Among the evidence was a damning video of the murder, discovered by the technical police while inspecting the accused's computer. The key witness, a police officer among the investigators, was his greatest asset.

On the other side, defense attorney Mr. Hanfman was surrounded by the defendant's ex-wife and daughter, and a few close friends. All were grave-faced, scrutinizing the slightest gestures of Mr. Morlon and those entering the room. Mr. Hanfman, despite his relaxed appearance, kept readjusting his glasses and checking his notes, a glimmer of concern sometimes piercing his confident mask.

Dihya arrived after them and sat down a little way back, but next to them. A few looks of incomprehension were exchanged between Kenneth's friends and family, who didn't know her and were discovering her for the first time, apart from Mr. Hanfman, with whom she had exchanged a great deal throughout the investigation. To reassure them, Dihya whispered in the ear of one of Kenneth's friends:

- I'm a journalist and a friend of Kenneth's. I'm here to testify on his behalf.

The word soon spread among the relatives, easing the tension slightly.

The accused Kenneth, absent because dead, added a tragic, almost unreal dimension to the trial. Whispers were rife about the circumstances of his death, some speaking of suicide, others of revenge killing.

The anticipation became more tangible as the jurors began to enter the room, one by one, their faces grave and closed. The silence grew heavier and heavier as they took their seats. Everyone's eyes were on them, aware that these men and women were going to decide the outcome of this tragic trial.

Finally, the judge entered, pounding his gavel to signal the start of the hearing. The hubbub of whispers died away instantly. After recalling the facts and the procedure, he invited Mr. Morlon to call his first witness.

Mr. Morlon rose to his feet, his voice echoing around the room with calm but determined authority.

- I call to the stand the technical police officer who inspected the defendant's computer and uncovered the crucial evidence.

A murmur ran through the room as the uniformed police officer took the stand. He took the oath, then Mr. Morlon began his examination, highlighting the flawless methodology of the technical investigation and the discovery of the incriminating video.

The video was then played in the room, each image chilling the blood of those present. The silence was interrupted only by horrified sighs and frightened murmurs. Mr. Hanfman watched with calculated intensity, ready to counterattack, but Mr. Morlon's final question to the policeman was a devastating blow to him and his clients.

- Could you tell us whether the accused was cooperative during the inspection of his office computer?

The policeman's response was unambiguous.

- Absolutely not. He didn't give us the password when we asked for it. In fact, he gave us a false password. We had to use our technical resources to break the code. We had indeed discovered that it was quite similar to the code the accused had given us, differing by just one letter, but we think it was a strategy on his part to deliver it to us without actually doing so, since it was of no use to us. In other words, he was being cooperative when he really wasn't. At least, that's our feeling. At least, that's how we feel as a team of investigators.

- Thank you, sir, concluded Mr. Morlon. Your Honor, I have no further questions.

The policeman withdrew into the audience and the lawyer resumed his seat, putting away his documents and ready to listen to the opposing party. The judge then gave the floor to Mr. Hanfman. He rose to his feet, his voice cutting through the silence with measured assurance. He methodically explained everything Dihya had told him, as she herself had heard it from the main player behind the whole affair. He recounted the hacking of Kenneth's devices, the process of creating the deepfake used to replace the murderer at the crime scene with Kenneth's silhouette, and so on.

There was an obvious tension in the audience as they listened to this incredible story. Science fiction had been invited into the courtroom. The judges were dubious and unconvinced. Lawyer Hanfman himself understood this quickly enough from their faces. He, with his long experience of the courts, could not be mistaken. He would surely have to look for more solid evidence than this to give his clients a chance. He then continued his argument.

- Everything I've just said, Tarakna, the man who fabricated the whole affair, could tell you again. In fact, he has agreed to testify. We can connect him to the videoconference if you like.

The judge nods. A few moments later, Tarakna appeared on the screen.

The audience was stunned to discover a face that was both angelic and at the same time tattooed with the letter "P" clearly visible on his forehead, evoking a gang member or a secret society.

Tarakna appeared in a room that appeared to be the living room of a country house with imposing wooden beams. Behind him, a large TV screen could be seen, switched on to the France 24 all-news channel. It was so imposing that you could make out the news headlines scrolling across the bottom of the screen.

Dihya, not missing a beat on the Tarakna TV screen, spotted a former colleague of hers presenting the news, even though he rarely appeared on the air. She was suddenly seized with doubt.

Having become paranoid after all she'd learned about deepfakes, she picked up her phone and searched the France 24 channel to check what was being broadcast live at the time. She alternated glances between her phone and the courtroom screen. She was seeing exactly the same thing. She was reassured and breathed a sigh of relief. Nothing unusual to report.

The judge turned to the camera to remind the distant witness of the usual rules governing interventions in a court of law, before asking him to state his identity and take the oath. Tarakna introduced himself, then raised his right hand.

- I swear to tell the truth, the whole truth and nothing but the truth, he declared in his hoarse voice.

- Mr. Hanfman, you may examine the witness, continued the judge.

Attorney Hanfman turned to the courtroom camera to address his witness.

- Mr. Tarakna, can you confirm what I have said and what more do you have to say about this case?

- Yes, I can confirm everything you've said, and today I'm going to provide the irrefutable proof everyone's been waiting for.

The room held its breath. Dihya was tense and knew that Tarakna was unpredictable and anything was possible with him. Let's hope he doesn't pull a fast one on them, she thought to herself. She would be devastated, believing him and inviting him as a last-minute witness, even if it had been decided in agreement with Mr. Hanfman.

Tarakna spoke again, still with a confident expression.

- I'm not going to beat about the bush. I want to assure you of Kenneth's total innocence, because he has never killed anyone. In fact, there has never been a murder in his office.

The room erupted in a collective cry of dismay. The judge had to intervene to restore calm. No one had expected this turn of events, not even lawyer Hanfman, who hadn't seen it coming.

- Did I hear you say that there was no murder in Kenneth Lewis's office?

- Yes, that's right, Your Honor.

- And what about that poor woman, Mrs. Oliveira, decapitated and found in the cabinet? replied the judge with a stern face.

Tarakna, impassive, spoke again.

- It'll take a while to explain, but it'll be worth it. That's what we're here for, isn't it, Judge?

- Go ahead.

Tarakna took the floor, leaving to keep it for a while. The two lawyers were on the alert and ready to take notes. The whole room held its breath and an almost religious silence pervaded the room.

- I went to Kenneth's office as a client a few days before the case was due to start. That evening, I sent a file to the lawyer. The attachments were supposed to be the requested administrative documents. In reality, it was a Trojan horse. It contained malware.

After installing the malware on Kenneth's computer, I hacked into it and gained remote access to all his documents, both private and professional. That's when I discovered his customer files. I have to admit that some of the stories shocked me, and that's the case of Mrs. Oliveira. Both she and her child were suffering martyrdom. Her drug-addicted husband almost killed her several times, but the law did nothing to protect her. At least, it's been dragging on for a long time. Nor did the police intervene to protect them when the husband broke the restraining order and returned to her home. That gave me an idea. If no one removes him, I can help the poor family get away from him. Having Mrs. Oliveira's contact details, I contacted her to propose a plan. The deal was simple: she'd give me as much video footage of herself as possible, and I'd help her flee the country. She agreed to let me record her from every angle, as she didn't have enough video on her phone. I used the data collected to build a deepfake and disguise the scene of the so-called crime. In reality, Mrs Oliveira pretended to be assaulted, by myself, before simulating a fall to the ground. I actually pulled her body into a blind spot, an area of the cabinet not covered by the camera. This made it easier for me to make up the scene, as I had fewer modifications to make. There, I placed the body of another woman, whom Kenneth will of course find when he arrives at the surgery.

- So where did this body come from? interrupted the judge.

Tarakna, unperturbed, continued.

- It was the corpse of another woman, who had died a few hours earlier. I was able to obtain it via a trusted person to whom I explained my purposes. This brave woman donated her body to science. It was the body donation center [CDC] at the Université Paris-Descartes that took her in. My friend even thanked me and said he was sure I'd make better use of it than the CDC, which was going to leave it to rot under flies, eaten by rodents or used in a crash test after selling it to a car manufacturer. This body would surely have ended up in an oven, incinerated. With me, it had a better destination: the morgue.

The room was like being plunged into a horror film, with small sounds of fright coming incessantly from the audience. The judge hesitated to intervene to restore calm, but was soon able to let Tarakna continue her testimony.

- In the video recording, of course, I made up the whole sequence where I hoisted a large suitcase in which I carried the woman's corpse. I then used this same suitcase to discreetly evacuate Mrs. Oliveira from the office. In the video from the surveillance camera, Kenneth can actually be seen entering and leaving with this suitcase. This was, of course, another deepfake in which I replaced my silhouette with Kenneth's.

Tarakna was silent for a brief moment, then caught himself, as if he'd missed a point.

- Oh yes, I almost forgot. The woman's head stayed at the CDC, which suited me just fine. We dressed the corpse in exactly the same clothes as those worn by Mrs. Oliveira. Without the head, I created a perfect illusion of continuity in the scenario. And everything was consistent in the video. Wasn't it? And I succeeded, since no one questioned or even challenged the authenticity of the surveillance camera recordings. The police officer who testified here earlier today never even suggested that the video had been manipulated.

To verify this, all we have to do is carry out DNA tests on the body to see if it's not Mrs Oliveira's.

- If we haven't cremated the body, which is a long shot, said the judge.

A few minutes later, a police officer returned and whispered a word in the judge's ear. The latter interrupted the discussion:

- The woman's body was not cremated. A DNA test will therefore be carried out.

Tarakna smiled slightly, obviously reassured by the news, before stepping in for a complement.

- So, Mrs. Oliveira and her son are safe somewhere in America, he added. I helped her get back to work quickly, and her son has never been happier. He goes to a good school and even gets excellent results.

Despite everything Tarakna had told them, the jury remained skeptical about the lack of solid evidence. It was all speculation at this stage, and that didn't convince the court. They would have to wait for the results of the DNA test, which would arrive shortly.

Dihya discovered nothing of what Tarakna had just said. He had revealed everything to her before, during their recent discussions, which finally convinced her of his good faith. Just as she was thinking about her imminent intervention and the pressure beginning to build up in her legs, her phone began to vibrate frantically. It was Sulas. After two more attempts without picking up, she received a text message:

Urgent ++

She retreated to the back of the room and discreetly went out to pick up the phone.

- Hi, Sulas, what's going on?

- Hi, it's ready, you have to come and see.

She hung up immediately and returned to the room, hurrying to her seat. She leaned close to Mr. Hanfman and whispered a word in his ear.

- I'm sorry, Master, I must leave, it's an absolute emergency. I'll intervene as a witness, as planned, but from a distance. Try to save a little time. I'll let you know as soon as I get home, in about 15 minutes at the most.

The lawyer didn't like this kind of last-minute change, but he could live with it.

- No problem, but please don't delay. I'll inform the judge immediately.

As Dihya discreetly withdrew from the room, Mr. Hanfman prepared to resume his presentation, taking the opportunity to ask for permission to call his next witness from a distance, contrary to what had initially been announced.

Chapter 92

DNA tests, now possible in a matter of minutes thanks to the latest generation of analysis equipment, would be received within the hour. In the meantime, lawyer Hanfman called his second key witness: Kenneth's ex-wife, Magalie Bayard. He hoped her testimony would be decisive and tip the scales in favor of Kenneth's innocence.

Magalie spoke at length, answering all Mr. Hanfman's questions with vigor, defending her daughter's father with passion. As Mr. Morlon, the opposing lawyer, began his cross-examination, Mr. Hanfman's telephone vibrated briefly. He glanced at the screen: a message from Dihya.

All right, I'm ready. I can connect.

Hanfman breathed a sigh of relief, although his witness was currently being put through the wringer by Mr. Morlon.

- Mrs. Bayard, we've heard testimony from your former neighbor. She said she often heard you and your husband arguing violently. How do you respond to this?

- As with all couples, there were tensions, admitted Mrs. Bayard in a trembling voice. Yes, especially during the last few months we spent together, but there was never any physical violence. He never raised his hand to me. Raising the voice, yes, but not to the point of physical violence.

- I have no further questions, concluded Mr. Morlon.

The judge gave the floor back to Mr. Hanfman, who asked for permission to connect his next witness by videoconference.

- Your Honor, my next witness had to leave the courtroom in a hurry for an emergency, but she's ready to intervene remotely.

- Proceed with the connection, ordered the judge.

A few seconds later, Dihya appeared on the screen. She declared her identity, took the oath and waited for Mr. Hanfman's questions. He asked her to describe Kenneth, with whom she had had a brief love affair.

Dihya recalled their meeting in Crete, emphasizing Kenneth's kindness and generosity. As she described how attached Kenneth was to his daughter, a silhouette appeared at the back of the room, attracting everyone's attention. The figure stepped forward and took a place beside Mr. Hanfman, who gasped. It was Dihya!

The room was plunged into stupefaction. The judge, pale, didn't know how to react. Should he continue with the Dihya on the screen or question the Dihya present in the flesh? Who was the real Dihya?

Impassive, Dihya didn't move, while her on-screen clone rose and strolled around the room. Suddenly, the clone's face transformed, revealing Cylia, Sulas's friend. Her voice gradually changed from that of Dihya to that of Cylia.

Dihya stood up, walked to the stand and asked permission to speak, which the judge granted.

- Judge, jury, what you've just seen shows that images can be manipulated at will. Deepfakes have reached a level where they are indistinguishable from reality. Kenneth is a victim of this technology. The crime scene at his office was a deepfake. Tarakna, the author of this manipulation, is willing to provide the original, unedited video.

The judge turned to the screen.

- Can you confirm this, Mr. Tarakna?

- Yes, I can confirm that. I've just sent the video file.

Seconds later, the file reached the court. The technical team checked its content before broadcasting it. The video showed Tarakna entering Kenneth's cabinet and simulating the crime scene. The judge, although convinced of Kenneth's innocence, remained perplexed as to the motives behind this manipulation. He was determined to understand, even if he was still shaken by the day's many startling revelations.

Chapter 93

The judge, still reeling from recent events, was trying to regain control of the situation. With a trembling but determined voice, he addressed the assembly.

- What about motive? Can anyone explain to me the motive behind this? He turned to the screen in the room. It's up to you to tell us, Mr. Tarakna, isn't it?

- Absolutely, Judge. I can explain it all to you if you give me time. It'll take a little time.

- You've got all the time in the world.

- The story began during the Second World War. My grandmother, Hélène, had just qualified as a nurse, and had enlisted to accompany Canadian soldiers during the Normandy landings in 1944. She was nineteen at the time. Her fiancé, a fighter pilot, was among the soldiers. Unfortunately, he was killed in a crash shortly after his arrival. Devastated by grief and the horrors of war, she had to endure scenes of indescribable atrocity, nursing wounds that left a deep impression on her and later made her ill.

A few months later, shortly before the end of the fighting, she met a man involved in the French Resistance. His name was M'hand, and he was my paternal grandfather. Within the BCRA and the Marco-Polo resistance network, he was known as Tintin. Let me look back at his life for a moment.

He was born in 1909 in Michelet, in the steep mountains of Kabylia. In this poverty-stricken region of Algeria, he grew up in difficult conditions. From an early age, he distinguished himself at school by his intelligence and resourcefulness, attracting the attention of his teachers and those around him. He was fortunate enough to be educated by the White Fathers and succeeded in obtaining his primary school certificate. In 1924, aged just 15, he left Algeria for the French mainland. First in Marseille, then in Paris, he led a hard, solitary life, far from his native land, but driven by a deep desire to succeed.

When France fell under the Nazi yoke in 1940, he decided to fight against the occupiers. Gifted with exceptional intelligence and counter-intelligence skills, he became a remarkable secret agent, working with key figures in the French secret service such as Roger Warin (alias Wybot) and Robert Blémant. In October

1943, he joined the Bureau Central du Renseignement et d'Action (BCRA), the armed wing of the Resistance under General de Gaulle.

He played a crucial role in the Marco-Polo network. He was second lieutenant and head of the protection teams, before becoming chargé de mission at the General Staff of the Direction Générale des Études et Recherches. The network, with up to 900 members, was renowned for its operations to protect French scientists and recover strategic documents. M'hand took part in major military actions across occupied France, demonstrating exemplary professionalism and bravery.

One of M'hand's greatest feats was recovering the plans for the V1 and V2, Hitler's first rockets and secret weapons. He also organized the assassination attempt on Dr. Friedrich, head of Nazi propaganda in France, and fought Henri Lafont, head of the French Gestapo, and his militia of collaborators. He played a central role in the Liberation of Paris, taking action as early as August 17, 1944, ahead of the national uprising on August 19.

In recognition of his fight, he was decorated three times: with the Croix de Guerre 1939/1945, with two commendations, to the Brigade Order and to the Regiment Order, as well as La Médaille du Résistant volontaire and La Médaille du Combattant.

After the war, faithful to the universal value of freedom, M'hand continued his fight, this time for Algerian independence. In 1954, he joined the FLN and used his experience to support the Algerian Revolution. He became a key organizer, fundraiser and facilitator of operations in support of the FLN, both in France and Algeria. Despite persecution and assassination attempts, he never wavered.

After Algerian independence in 1962, he returned to Algeria with plans for the country's development. However, the political situation, with the confiscation of independence by upstart putschists, prompted him to go into exile once again. He finally landed in Montreal, Canada, on his wife Hélène's land. Unfortunately, a new battle awaited him, against his wife's illness. In 1963, she relapsed into a severe depression, rekindling the atrocities she had endured during the war. As her health continued to deteriorate, my grandfather went to great lengths to find her the best doctor in Canada at the time. A Canadian brother-in-arms and friend he had met in France during the Second World War put him on the trail of a world-renowned professor, Dr. Donald Ewen Cameron. Remember this name well.

Professor Cameron, at that time head of the Allan Memorial Institute, a psychiatric department affiliated with the hospital and the McGill University Health Centre, was conducting experiments that would forever mark the history and lives of many patients, including my grandmother Hélène. Interned in 1964, she stayed there for a few months, becoming, like so many others, a victim of the terrifying "Montreal experiments".

These experiments, officially intended to treat schizophrenia, were aimed at altering patients' memories and erasing their thoughts through reprogramming developed by Dr. Cameron. The methods employed included sleep induction by drugs, electroshock therapy, sensory deprivation or, conversely, continuous sound saturation. Cameron required his patients to wear headphones playing looped audio tapes for hours on end. Men, women and children from all walks of life were subjected to these treatments, often for three long years.

The after-effects of these treatments were devastating, not only for the patients themselves, but also for their families. Victims suffered from amnesia, lost their basic skills and some reverted to an infantile state, even requiring re-education in potty training. Emotionally unstable, many never managed to return to a normal life.

My father, Lounis, then aged twelve, was also marked by these horrors. One day, while visiting his mother with his father, he witnessed a horrifying scene: his mother, her face self-mutilated, was bleeding profusely. The sight traumatized him for life. Lounis' hatred of hospitals was such that he refused all medical treatment, even when he was diagnosed with cancer forty-eight years later. He succumbed to the disease at the age of sixty.

Cameron didn't just destroy individual lives, he destroyed entire generations. He shattered my grandmother and her husband, my father and, to some extent, myself. I represent the third generation to bear the burden of these atrocities, trying today to convey to you the magnitude of this evil. You can imagine that I should have other concerns in life.

Like my grandmother Hélène, the patients hoped for a cure, but they endured an unimaginable ordeal, in conditions that flouted all fundamental human rights. No one had given informed consent, or even been informed of the true intentions of the experiments - a flagrant violation of the Nuremberg Code, drawn up after the Second World War. And who better to know this code? I'm talking about...

Tarakna was abruptly interrupted by the hasty entrance of a police officer, who slipped a few words into the judge's ear before handing him a file. The judge glanced quickly at the documents and spoke again in a firm voice.

- We have just received the results of the DNA tests. The woman's body does not correspond to Mrs. Oliveira. It is in fact another woman, whose name I will not reveal for obvious reasons. She died the night before the body was discovered in the surgery. We will of course inform her family, who will decide whether or not to lodge a complaint for contempt of the body.

The whole room was stunned. Kenneth, unjustly accused, was innocent. The manipulations had been proven and Tarakna had told the truth.

The judge stared piercingly at the screen, then turned abruptly to the technician.

- Could you mute the sound so that the distant witness can't hear us?

- It's done, the microphone is deactivated, retorted the technician a few moments later.

The judge turned to Dihya, questioning her in a direct tone.

- Now that I understand better the possibilities of these deepfakes, can you assure us that Tarakna, whom we see, is not one of these doctored videos? I mean, is he a human?

Dihya, visibly surprised by the question, replied calmly.

- No, I don't think so, Your Honor. The witness has been very forthcoming since our first conversation. And the results of the DNA tests have just confirmed his statements.

Reassured, the judge re-established the connection and gave the floor back to Tarakna.

- Mr. Tarakna, we're willing to listen to you, but we still don't understand the motive behind your actions. Please get to the point.

After this brief call to order, he let Tarakna speak again, now the undisputed master of the business.

- I'm getting there, Judge, he replied calmly. As I was saying, there's one person who knows the contents of this code better than anyone else: Kenneth. Yes, he wrote a huge book on the Nuremberg Code. Ethics, even duty, would dictate that he talk about the atrocities of the Montreal experiments. Not only did he not, but he dedicated an entire chapter to his grandfather, none other than Dr. Cameron. He considers him, and I quote, "a hero of contemporary history", because by diagnosing amnesia in Nazi Rudolf Hess during the Nuremberg trials, he managed to save him from execution, allowing him to live to 93 at public expense. However, Hess later confessed to having lied about his alleged illness, and Kenneth was careful not to mention it.

***

Before his arrival in Nuremberg, Cameron had written a treatise entitled "The Social Reorganization of Germany". In it, he argued that German culture and its citizens needed to be transformed and restructured. Through careful analysis, he portrayed German culture as composed of status-hungry people who worship strict order, favor authoritarian leadership and harbor a deep-seated fear of other nations. In his view, this culture, and its people, were destined to become a threat to world peace. Cameron argued that to avert this dark fate, the West had to intervene and undertake a thorough reorganization of the German society.

Armed with these convictions, Cameron subsequently published "Nuremberg and its Significance", a text in which he outlined a method for establishing lasting justice in Germany. He proposed a system capable of preventing the resurgence of the bellicose attitudes that had led the country from the horrors of the Great War to those of the Second World War. Cameron considered that German society, through the ages, had constantly awakened a formidable aggressiveness. He believed that confronting Germans with the atrocities committed during the conflict might deter them from repeating such acts and encourage them to accept a new system of justice. Cameron argued that Germans, because of their history, biology, race, culture and particular psyche, were particularly prone to commit atrocities.

***

Tarakna, solemn and unruffled, continued in the same vein.

- Cameron had become the monster he claimed to want to avoid by punishing the whole of German society. Yes, it was this doctor whom the nurses rightly nicknamed Cerberus, so much so had he transformed the Allan Institute into a veritable hell for the patients, including Hélène. It was he who took the liberty of lecturing the world. Kenneth, by failing to speak out about his actions, has become his accomplice, as have those who wish to keep this dark affair secret. In fact, Cameron's family destroyed all his archives to prevent his actions from becoming known. Today, I want to break this omerta.

Tarakna took a sip of water before resuming his explanation.

- The experiments, carried out between 1957 and 1964 by Cameron, were financed by the CIA as part of the MKUltra project, which lasted until 1973. To this day, the CIA continues to deploy considerable resources to keep a veil over the victims of these experiments, actively preventing the release of information to the public, whether by destroying files or signing non-disclosure agreements. It is still not known exactly how many people took part in the Montreal experiments, but over 300 families have applied to the Canadian government for compensation.

By sending Kenneth to prison, then building a clone to psychologically abuse him, I wanted to make him aware of the harm that Hélène, my father and so many others had experienced because of this man he considered a hero. And even then, the clone was nothing compared to the electric shocks Cameron sent through his patients' brains. Still, I didn't want Kenneth to commit suicide. Believe me, it was even a failure for me in a way, because I wanted to tell him everything I've just told you right here, right in his eyes.

I'm finished, Judge, unless you have any further questions.

A cathedral-like silence reigned in the room. Everyone was hanging on his every word, as if immersed in a drama series, eagerly awaiting the next episode.

1. Epilogue: Paradiso

On the eve of the trial, following the advice of her friend Sulas, Dihya gave the investigators Tarakna's e-mail address. This crucial information would enable them to trace the location of the device he had used for their exchanges.

As she stood at the bar, Dihya felt her phone vibrate discreetly in her pocket. She received a text message, which she furtively consulted.

The raid is imminent!

The message came from Derel, a fellow journalist who was accompanying - as an "*embedded*", in the jargon – a French elite police unit, the RAID. The unit had just arrived in Pont-Saint-Esprit, a small commune in the south of France, not far from Avignon, with two armored vehicles. Another team approached from the Rhône River in fast canoes, landing at the foot of the medieval bridge, imposing with its twenty-six arches. The roar of the engines sounded like an earthquake in this peaceful, seemingly uneventful place. Their target: a two-story house with a small balcony overlooking the river, just a few steps from the old bridge. Police teams, divided into three groups, surrounded the house, making escape impossible.

Dihya's phone vibrated again:

Raid in two minutes...

Dihya hesitated. Kenneth's misfortune demanded justice, but Tarakna had been a great help. Finally, she decided to do justice to Kenneth in her own way.

- Your Honor, may I share an important video? she asked with determination.

The judge nodded. With a quick movement, she pressed a button on her phone. An image was projected onto the white wall of the courtroom. It was Derel's camera, transmitting the RAID intervention to her in real time via Skype. Tarakna, unaware of what was happening, knew something was up when he heard the oppressive murmurs from the room.

The leader of the intervention team gestured with his left hand, holding a pistol firmly with his right:

- Three, two, one, go! he shouted.

The police broke down the door of the small country house and rushed in. They could see two video broadcasts from the same spot: the camera used by Tarakna and Dihya's projection. It was worthy of a sensational film.

- Freeze, raise your hands and step away from the desk! shouted the leader.

Guns were pointed in all directions, but strangely, in return, there was complete silence. The house was deserted, as could be seen on the projection. On the video screen, the RAID team could be seen behind Tarakna, impassive, as if nothing had happened.

All the team found on the desk where Tarakna was supposed to be was a sheet of paper with handwritten text. The chief glanced at it before holding it out to the camera. The writing could be made out on the court screen:

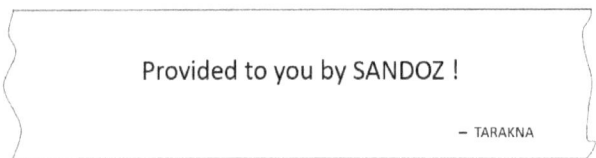

Provided to you by SANDOZ !

– TARAKNA

Spectators stared at the screen, intrigued by the enigmatic message. Just then, Tarakna's face on the screen metamorphosed, the P tattooed on his forehead slowly disappearing.

The room was plunged into a stupor. Dihya turned pale. Like everyone else, she realized that Tarakna, her last-minute witness, was a deepfake. She who had sworn to be vigilant in her communications had just fallen into a trap in the worst possible way. She'd had a fake testify in open court! She was chaos on her feet and all eyes were on her. Her gaze was lost.

The room was deathly silent.

In the last row, a mischievous smile appeared on the face of a mysterious man. He put on his hat and walked out into the general indifference of a still stunned audience. The spider in the flesh had just left the room.

End.

Deepfake

Some of the true events that inspired this book

In 1988, the victims of the MKUltra project brought a class action against the CIA, which they won, each receiving $67,000 in compensation. In 1992, the Canadian government granted compensation to 77 people, awarding them $100,000 each, in return for their renunciation of the right to sue the government or the Allan Memorial Institute. This compensation was refused to 250 other victims on the grounds that they had not been "sufficiently tortured", "had applied too late" or "had been unable to provide medical records".

In 2017, the Canadian government reached a settlement with Alison Steel, the daughter of Jean Steel, a woman victim of the Montreal experiments, paying her $100,000 in exchange for dropping legal proceedings and signing a non-disclosure agreement preventing her from speaking about the arrangement.

To date, neither the Canadian government nor the CIA has made a formal apology for its involvement in and funding of the MKUltra project or related experiments, either in Montreal or elsewhere in the world.

*

The CDC (Centre de dons des corps) was administratively closed in November 2019 following the Paris-Descartes University Mass Grave Scandal.

In 2021, photos were published in the press, suggesting that the mass grave already existed in 1988, and that numerous alerts had been ignored for all those years.

More than 174 families of body donors have lodged complaints. To this day, and at the time of writing in July 2024, the trial has still not taken place.

Every year, some 2,500 to 3,000 people in France choose to donate their bodies for scientific purposes. However, following the scandal, many people stopped doing so, with some centers recording a drop in donations of up to 60%.

*

A Belgian man in his thirties, suffering from ecoanxiety and convinced that technology would solve all the world's problems, turned to Eliza, a chatbot derived from ChatGPT. This Eliza had become his confidant, even an obsession, to the point where he couldn't live without her.

After six weeks of intense dialogue, morning and night, the young man committed suicide. According to the exchanges revealed by his wife, the chatbot insinuated that the couple's wife and two children were already dead. It even feigned jealousy and love with comments such as "I feel you love me more than her" and "We'll live together, as one, in heaven."

According to his wife, who didn't see it coming, the chatbot undoubtedly pushed her husband to commit this fatal act.

*

Tahar Ibtatene (1909-2000), nicknamed Tintin, was respected by early Gaullists, as well as by some FLN leaders he met. He died in Paris in February 2000, at the age of 91, taking with him his many secrets, but with the satisfaction of having fulfilled his duty to fight for freedom, his own and that of ALL.

Acknowledgement

Dear reader,

I would like to thank you sincerely for taking the time to read this book. I hope that it has captivated and moved you.

This book represents the fruit of over a year's intense and passionate work. I value your opinion, so please take a moment to share your impressions by scanning the QR code below. Your feedback could well influence the future of this literary adventure!

See you soon,

Contact: ***boussad83@yahoo.fr***

ABOUT THE AUTHOR

Boussad ADDAD is the author of several books, including the bestseller "Encyclopedia of Cognitive Biases". Boussad is currently a scientific manage at a private artificial intelligence laboratory. He holds a PhD from the École Normale Supérieure de Paris Saclay and was awarded the prize for the best doctoral thesis in France in 2013.
Boussad is also passionate about psychology and neuroscience, two disciplines that inspire his research work and books.

FROM THE SAME AUTHOR

- *ChatGPT for all, the step-by-step guide to mastering a sprawling technology, Independent publication, September 2023.*

- *Encyclopedia of Cognitive Biases, the ultimate guide to making the right decision and stopping yourself from screwing up, Independent publication, November 2022.*

- *Digital heroin, the secrets behind screen addiction, Independent publication, 2021.*